The Pre-existence
of Christ
in the New Testament

The Pre-existence of Christ
in the New Testament

FRED B. CRADDOCK

Abingdon Press ♪ *Nashville and New York*

THE PRE-EXISTENCE OF CHRIST IN THE NEW TESTAMENT

To
Nettie Lee

Preface

Christology lies very near, if not at the center of, current theological discussions. This can be explained in a general way, of course, by saying that Christology is central to the Christian faith. However, it is more directly helpful to say that Christology lies at the heart of the New Testament, and the New Testament has been, in our time, more directly and specifically a concern of theologians than is usually the case. This is to say that in the last twenty-five years, theology has wrestled not simply with biblical ideas or themes, but with the terms, the categories, the very language of the Scriptures. The nature of this enterprise made it inevitable that the principal issue would be hermeneutics; the nature of the materials under investigation made it inevitable that the principal topic would be Christology.

These endeavors have been welcomed by those who have been painfully aware that the distance between themselves and the New Testament is more than chronological: it is cultural, psychological, and intellectual as well as theological. How are virgin birth, transfiguration, resurrection, and ascension to be understood? Honesty with the material demands these not be swept under the rug; honesty with self demands that one not pretend to believe what is at the same time regarded as incredible. And at no point does this problem more sharply arise than in the effort of intelligent faith to appropriate the affirmations of the pre-existence of Christ.

This book is an investigation of this one dimension of New Testament Christology. Interest in the subject arose during seminary days among the pains of growing faith, but earnest pursuit of the matter began in graduate studies under Dr. Leander Keck and the late Dr. Kendrick Grobel of the Divinity School of Vanderbilt University. The fruit of those studies was a dissertation on the Christological hymn in Colossians 1:15-20, which contributed method, incentive, and sizable content to this exploration into the meaning of the pre-existence of Christ in the New Testament.

I wish to express my indebtedness to Dr. Keck for his invaluable guidance. If there is merit in the book, much credit is due him; the inadequacies are my own. I am also indebted to the Graduate Seminary of Phillips University and to its dean, Dr. Daniel Joyce, for encouraging me to resume this work after a fire had destroyed an earlier draft of the manuscript.

FRED B. CRADDOCK

Enid, Oklahoma

Contents

Introduction:
Problem and Procedure

This book asks the reader to share in an investigation of the meaning of the pre-existence of Christ as it is expressed in the New Testament. This is an invitation to join in an exploration that may seem strange, perhaps even unreal, in that it focuses upon a category of being that does not correspond to reality as we experience it. In fact, the word "pre-existence" does not fit comfortably in the vocabulary of Western man. It has an exotic ring. It seems a fugitive word, escaped from a séance, wandering among us but not at home on the well-lighted streets of our empirical thoughts. It is not that we are unfamiliar with the word. We are—at least, with the idea. On various levels of seriousness, from superstition to philosophy, the category of pre-existence has been mediated to us.

On the popular level, fragments of the idea lie like broken pieces of jade upon the edge of our memory of stories from

Kipling's India. An exchange student from the Orient explains his way of life with references to pre-existence and reincarnation. A housewife breaks the boredom of her kitchen sink with "memories" of a former life of excitement in the highlands of Scotland. A mother, long childless, whispers lullabies over the cradle of the baby which has come "from above" to be hers "for awhile." An eccentric shares with story-starved reporters vivid recollections of having lived "another time, another place."

On a deeper level, the poetry of William Wordsworth introduced many in our culture to the category of pre-existence. Every schoolboy has had his mind stretched by those strangely beautiful lines:

> Our birth is but a sleep and a forgetting:
> The Soul that rises with us, our life's Star,
>   Hath had elsewhere its setting,
>   And cometh from afar:
>   Not in entire forgetfulness,
>   And not in utter nakedness,
> But trailing clouds of glory do we come
>   From God, who is our home.[1]

On the deepest levels of theological reflection, the category of pre-existence has often been employed in treatments of the nature of man. For some Christian thinkers the doctrine of the pre-existence of the soul adequately accounts for man's

---

[1] "Ode: Intimations of Immortality from Recollections of Early Childhood."

power of self-transcendence and his kinship with the Divine. That the human spirit was created by God in eternity before time began was a fundamental tenet in Origen's theology. Similarly, the American transcendentalist Ralph Waldo Emerson explained the soul's intuition of the Eternal: "The soul of man, embodied here on earth, went roaming up and down in quest of that other world of its own out of which it came into this." [2] This thesis was more recently taken up by Nicolas Berdyaev, for whom human personality begins not at conception or birth but in eternity. This preterrestrial history conditions the terrestrial existence of every human spirit.[3]

Most, if not all, of these reflections upon pre-existence, at whatever level they have been mediated to our culture, draw upon the philosophy of Plato. His definition of learning as memory extended his thought to the dimension of pre-existence.

Since the soul is immortal and often born, having seen what is in the home of Hades, and everything, there is nothing it has not learnt; so there is no wonder it can remember about virtue and other things, because it knew about these before.[4]

---

[2] Essay on "Love."

[3] Matthew Spinka, *Nicolas Berdyaev* (Philadelphia: Westminster, 1950), pp. 129-30. References to Berdyaev's *Destiny of Man* (New York: Harper, 1959) are found on pp. 79, 86, 324, 328 and to his *Meaning of History* (Gloucester, Mass.: Peter Smith) on pp. 39-41, 44-45.

[4] "Meno," *Great Dialogues of Plato,* trans. W. H. D. Rouse (New York: New American Library, 1956), p. 42.

Or again, "Our souls existed long ago, before they were in human shape, apart from bodies, and then had wisdom." [5]

No doubt the contemporary mind, poised over a cup of tea, continues to enjoy playing with these ideas, tempering its play with the degree of seriousness appropriate to popular superstitions, poet's dreams, theologian's reflections, or philosopher's musings. But if that mind be Christian, or in serious dialogue with Christianity, then the category of preexistence insists upon being admitted into the chambers of that mind reserved for grappling with truth and ultimate reality. Anyone who would seriously consider Jesus Christ must seriously consider the New Testament affirmations of his pre-existence.

In the beginning was the Word, and the Word was with God, and the Word was God. . . . And the Word became flesh and dwelt among us. (John 1:1, 14a)

Truly, truly, I say to you, before Abraham was, I am. (John 8:58)

Father, glorify thou me in thy own presence with the glory which I had with thee before the world was made. (John 17:5)

Yet for us there is one God, the Father, from whom are all things and for whom we exist, and one Lord, Jesus Christ, through whom are all things and through whom we exist. (I Cor. 8:6)

For they [the Israelites] drank from the supernatural Rock which followed them, and the Rock was Christ. (I Cor. 10:4)

---

[5] *Ibid.,* p. 480.

For you know the grace of our Lord Jesus Christ, that though he was rich, yet for your sake he became poor, so that by his poverty you might become rich. (II Cor. 8:9)

Who, though he was in the form of God, did not count equality with God a thing to be grasped, but emptied himself, taking the form of a servant, being born in the likeness of men. (Phil. 2:6-7)

He is the image of the invisible God, the first-born of all creation; for in him all things were created. . . . He is before all things, and in him all things hold together. (Col. 1:15, 16a, 17)

In these last days he has spoken to us by a Son, whom he appointed the heir of all things, through whom also he created the world. (Heb. 1:2)

He [Moses] considered abuse suffered for the Christ greater wealth than the treasures of Egypt. (Heb. 11:26)

I am the Alpha and the Omega, the first and the last, the beginning and the end. (Rev. 22:13)

These, as well as other more veiled affirmations of his preexistence, form such a significant part of the New Testament portrait of Christ [6] that a casual dismissal of these statements as "prescientific" is hardly an adequate response. Whether or

---

[6] Of course, the word "pre-existence" does not occur in the NT. It comes from the Latin *prae-existentia*. The Neo-Platonists used the category "before being." Cf. E. A. Sophocles, *Greek Lexicon of the Roman and Byzantine Periods* (3rd ed.; New York: Frederick Ungar, 1957), II, 934. Ignatius expressed the temporal force of the idea of pre-existence: above or beyond time (Magnesians 6:1; Polycarp 3:2). The earliest use I have found of the term "pre-existent" to refer to Christ is in Justin Martyr's *Dialogue with Trypho* 48.

not pre-existence remains in the language and thought structures of the Christian's creed, this idea and the doctrines framed upon it must be dealt with honestly.

But this very honesty demands an admission at the outset that we are not at home with the category of pre-existence. This uneasiness, expressed in the opening paragraph, is, in fact, one reason prompting this investigation. It would probably be helpful at this point to remind ourselves of more specific reasons for our intellectual discomfort with this dimension of traditional Christology.

In the first place, our civilization takes history seriously and within history finds meaning and value.[7] This is to say that life is viewed in terms of time, having beginning and end. This framework is considered the valid structure within which the histories of men and institutions are to be understood, and to speak of a person or institution as having had an existence prior to the parenthesis of history is foreign and confusing. In some areas of the Orient, however, the cyclical view of life not only permits but demands the category of pre-existence, and what the Western mind regards as the "line" of history is for some Oriental minds but an "arc," a fraction of the great circle that has moved into view.

A second reason for difficulty in understanding pre-existence is the fact that the biblical materials, through which the concept comes to be a matter of concern for us, arose in

---

[7] To be discussed in chapter III. In more extreme forms of a historical approach to reality there is no room for statements about reality apart from discoverable history.

the Near East, where Occident and Orient meet in the fusion of two world views. While the Judeo-Christian tradition is rather clearly fixed upon the linear view of history, it has been influenced by the cyclical view. Although in this tradition the idea of the pre-existence (existence in a former stage) of human souls remained marginal,[8] pre-existence as a category of thought was employed, as will be noted in chapter I, in a variety of ways. However, the concept of pre-existence has one meaning in terms of the historical line, but quite a different meaning in terms of the eternal cycle. In the one case pre-existence carries a temporal force, "prior to," whereas in the other it means "suprahistorical," implying not only "prior to" but "subsequent to" history.

A third reason for confusion is a consequence of the second; that is, the dictionary offers no solution but merely records the confusion. *Webster's New International Dictionary, Second Edition,* permits pre- to signify priority in time, space, or rank. Thus, for example, a pre-existent Christ with reference to creation might be temporally defined as one having existence prior to the *act* of creation. However, creation refers not simply to the act of creating but to that which has been created. Therefore, in relation to the act, pre-existence carries a strong temporal connotation, but in relation to the created

---

[8] Some commentators regard John 9:1 as a reflection of the doctrine of the pre-existence of souls. See more clearly in Wis. of Sol. 8:19, 20 (Apocrypha, RSV). For references to the treasury (*guf*) where souls were kept and the pre-existence of the souls of the righteous and the patriarchs, ideas rather prominent in apocalyptic and mystical circles of Judaism and in some rabbis, cf. "Pre-existence," *The Jewish Encyclopedia* (New York: Funk & Wagnalls, 1905), X, 182-84.

universe as such, pre-existence could easily carry the connotation of "pre-eminence," "priority in rank," "superiority over," "noncontingency." Immediately, therefore, the idea of pre-existence in such a discussion could carry the double force of involvement in creation as a process and yet pre-eminence over creation as a product. The prepositions "before" and "above" both might be used to convey these meanings.

A final reason for confusion with reference to the concept of pre-existence lies in the ambiguity of language; when a being is spoken of as pre-existent, is this to be taken as personification, or as a divine attribute hypostatically conceived and hence having independent existence, or as myth? [9] One person may speak of pre-existence and have in mind ideal existence in the mind of God; another may, in the same wording, refer to projections in the form of cosmic myths of man's self-understanding; yet another may have listened to the first two and thought they were in agreement concerning the actual, objective existence of a being who precedes and/or transcends the created order.

Lexicography, therefore, leaves us this legacy with which to begin this study: pre-existence, especially as applied to Christ, may refer to the existence of his soul prior to his physical conception; the existence of the Messiah in the mind of God; the existence of the Messiah in the heavenly realm before his advent; the eternal existence of Christ; the pre- and supratemporal existence of the agent of creation; the heav-

---

[9] Perhaps the point at which this debate is most clearly focused is in the efforts to understand the portrayal of Wisdom in Wis. of Sol.

enly rather than earthly man; the transhistorical as well as eternal rational principle in the universe; God himself in one of his many modes of action; the Christ whose incarnation was the acme of many epiphanies.

Quite obviously no serious investigation would attempt to sustain throughout the study this hopelessly confusing array of meanings. It is necessary, therefore, to establish some criterion (or criteria) for understanding the affirmation of the pre-existence of Christ.

One possibility is to select arbitrarily one of the meanings of the concept and apply that to the New Testament affirmations. All passages could be enlisted that reflected the definition given, and all others that "seemed" to affirm pre-existence could be explained otherwise or left unnoticed. Even so, by what canon would that one definition be determined, and what purpose would be served by such an isolated and narrow study? After all, the desire is to have the New Testament speak, not to speak to the New Testament (except to ask it questions).

Another possibility, and a far more favorable one, would be to move behind the New Testament affirmations to their tributaries, to the formulations of pre-existence in the background materials. It is generally recognized that the thought patterns and key terms in the New Testament presentations of Christ as pre-existent belonged to the religious and cultural milieu. The affinities appear self-evident in the common usage of significant terms. It would seem, then, that a knowledge of the meaning of these terms in these background materials would thus supply definitions for New Testament

19

studies in Christology. This method of understanding New Testament affirmations and, in particular, Christological statements on the basis of possible sources has a great deal of merit.

That we have available an abundance of such materials related by vocabulary, ideas, and literary forms to the New Testament expressions pertaining to Christ's person and work is due primarily to the monumental work of the comparative religion school, and especially to R. Reitzenstein.[10] Not even the sharpest critics of this approach to Christianity, and to Paul in particular, can fail to feel a debt of gratitude for the amassing of materials that enlighten New Testament language and liturgy. In fact, one is likely to be so overwhelmed by the collection of data that the failures of the approach will be overlooked. These are primarily three: first, the predisposition to interpret Paul (a major source of affirmations of Christ's pre-existence) Hellenistically rather than Judaistically eliminates proper consideration of apocalyptic and rabbinic materials as well as the conservatism of Paul; second, Paul the syncretist completely obscures Paul the creative, dynamic, charismatic, and developing thinker;[11] and third (and this is fatal), this approach fails to regard the concrete condition or problem addressed by a particular passage. True,

---

[10] Cf. esp. his *Die hellenistischen Mysterienreligionen* (3rd ed.; Leipzig: B. G. Teubner, 1927).

[11] For this failure, Albert Schweitzer leveled against Reitzenstein two sharp sentences: "Before the poor apostle can get in a word, he has overwhelmed him with a shower of parallel passages from Hellenistic literature." "Paul . . . is, in fact, so travestied into the Professor that he retains scant resemblance to the Paul we meet in the letters." (*The Mysticism of Paul the Apostle*, trans. William Montgomery [2nd ed.; London: A. & C. Black, 1953], pp. 27, 28.)

these studies did not claim to be commentaries, but a consideration of the concerns of the readers, and the attempt of the writer to speak to those concerns, is irreplaceable in any investigation of a man through his correspondence[12] or of an idea within that correspondence. It is an unhappy experience to seek to understand I Corinthians with only a list of references from Philo, the Wisdom Literature, the Basilidians, and others. This method of definition by source seems always to stand outside the materials and thereby to convert existential concerns into academic speculations.

The work of W. L. Knox represents a correction of the extremes of comparative religion and yet offers an example of an investigator standing outside his material. In his work on Paul, Knox did not avoid the rabbinic and apocalyptic material, nor did he respect the gulf between Palestinian and Diaspora Judaism made artificially wide and deep by the century-old debate over whether Paul was Jew or Greek.[13] However, Knox sees Paul's thought, and especially his Christology, shaped by his desire to make Christianity intellectually respectable in the philosophical climate of the Hellenistic world. Knox thinks he can discern the time and place of

---

[12] Under the influence of this method, critical commentaries became compilations of references often without a guiding thought or any attempt to grasp the writer's purpose or the reader's condition.

[13] For a study of the history of that debate up to the early twentieth century see Schweitzer's *Paul and His Interpreters,* trans. William Montgomery (London: A. & C. Black, 1912). One must remember that the debaters are handled with special reference to whether or not they saw Paul primarily in the light of late Jewish Apocalyptic and its eschatology, Schweitzer's own position.

Paul's incorporation of the concept of pre-existence (meaning for Knox an orientation toward the beginning rather than end of the world) into his Christology: "His [Paul's] visit to Athens had shown that the emphasis must be transferred from the end of all things to the beginning if the educated Greek world was to be won for the Gospel, and he was perfectly aware of the necessity when he arrived in Corinth." [14] Knox's Paul, therefore, replaces "the awkward figure of the Messiah" with Sophia and Logos because "the Greek world demanded a consistent scheme of thought; and if Paul was pressed to provide one, he could only do so by assigning to Jesus a position in the order of reality which could scarcely be made acceptable to the unitarian monotheism of Judaism." [15] The image of Paul thus conveyed is that of a clever and adaptable but weak man, controlled by the thoughts and concepts of the intellectuals and philosophers in his audience. Knox has no basis in Paul's letters for these audiences of philosophers (certainly not Corinth or Colossae) as Knox understands philosophy, and he too easily extracts Paul's eschatological interests. Knox leans too much on Acts 17 and too little on Paul's correspondence for his image of Paul's audiences and their concerns. His approach, and hence his product, are too academic, for the reference to Athens moved Knox toward sources that defined Paul and his Christology in the Athenian spirit.

This approach to Paul's Christology, especially as it involves

---

[14] *St. Paul and the Church of the Gentiles* (New York: Macmillan, 1939), p. 111.

[15] *Ibid.*, p. 110.

the idea of pre-existence, indicates the inadequacy of definition by source[16] and common terminology, an inadequacy born of taking a stance outside the particular concerns and problems related to the particular use of an idea or term within a text. However, this is not meant to imply that this approach and its attendant fault belong solely to those who have emphasized the Hellenistic background of Paul. On the contrary, studies relating Paul more closely to the Old Testament canon and to rabbinic Judaism may be equally deaf to the existential questions and conditions of the readers and the particular intent of the writer. The primary difference is that most of the source references are drawn from the Hebrew canon and the Talmud rather than from the Hellenistic and Oriental materials. Two examples will suffice.

The work of Oscar Cullmann begins with two fundamental presuppositions, one theological and the other methodological. First, New Testament Christology must be understood in terms of *Heilsgeschichte*, the line of redemptive history running through primal history, discoverable history, and eschatological history.[17] Cullmann feels this is not the imposition of an external dogmatic scheme upon the material but is a method offered by the New Testament itself.[18] Second,

---

[16] Of course, the additional problem of actually determining a specific source for a word, concept, or myth is in many cases apparently insoluble. It is one thing to trace the background of Logos "in general," but another to say "this particular" writer's use of it lies in the immediate background of a NT text.

[17] *Christ and Time*, trans. Floyd Filson (rev. ed.; Philadelphia: Westminster, 1964), pp. 96-106.

[18] *Christology of the New Testament*, trans. S. C. Guthrie and C. A. M. Hall (rev. ed.; Philadelphia: Westminster, 1964), p. 315.

Cullmann is committed to the philological-historical method.[19] His *Christology of the New Testament* is a clear example of these two presuppositions guiding his investigation. The first presupposition not only permits him to "level" the New Testament,[20] but also predisposes him to favor background materials primarily Jewish because these materials, not Hellenistic philosophy and Gnostic mythology, are structured upon a time line. The second presupposition commits him to word studies and finely drawn word associations that are often overdrawn to the point of building a doctrinal superstructure upon one word.[21]

In his *Christology*, Cullmann makes his analysis of titles applied to Jesus, and one section is devoted to titles referring to Christ's pre-existence. A careful study of terms in the New Testament and in background materials is given, but an adequate recognition of variety in usage, an investigation of the problem addressed, and a discussion of the writer's intent are lacking, even though Cullmann has said such matters should receive attention.[22] For example, in his treatment of Phil. 2:6-11, Cullmann finds Son of Man, Servant of God, and Kyrios Christology. Since, he says, these can be under-

---

[19] "I know no other 'method' than the proven philological-historical one" (*Ibid.*, p. xiv).

[20] The variety Cullmann promised in his introduction, pp. 6-7, and said was present in his conclusion, pp. 315-16, is never brought into focus except as the titles themselves represent variety, but these titles are traced throughout the NT in a "level" fashion.

[21] Cf. *Ibid.*, pp. 174-81 for the treatment of Phil. 2:5-11. If this judgment here seems unfair, note also his study of Rom. 13:1 in *The State in the New Testament* (rev. ed.; New York: Scribner, 1966), pp. 95-114.

[22] *Christology*, p. 5.

stood only in the light of the Old Testament and Judaism, and since in those sources these titles refer to the Messiah, this passage is considered in the chapters dealing with the present and future work of Jesus, not his pre-existence. After all, the category of pre-existence is not native to the Messiah! His mention of pre-existence in the passage is brief and unclear, very likely because the pattern for the thought is the descent-ascent of the Redeemer and not chronological points on his preferred time line. The problems at Philippi, Paul's purpose, the indications in the letter as to the nature of the agitators in the church—these are passed by.[23] Cullmann's method in handling Christology is little different; he merely uses different sources for defining terms.

As Cullmann's method in Christology is philological, W. D. Davies' method may be called, perhaps oversimply, logical. With rabbinic Judaism as the frame of reference for understanding Paul,[24] Davies points to the centrality of the Torah for the rabbis, and presumably for Paul before his conversion. He marshals the references that speak of the Torah as pre-existent, as instrument of creation, as the historical concretization of Wisdom, and as related to Logos and Memra in some of the literature. It follows, then, that since for the converted Paul, Christ was central,[25] as formerly the Torah

---

[23] On the positive side I appreciate in Cullmann's work a respect for the historical and the grounding of theology in exegesis in a time when the desire for relevance and contemporaneity has oriented much of theology away from the Bible, an unnecessary and unfortunate shift.

[24] *Paul and Rabbinic Judaism* (2nd ed.; London: SPCK, 1955).

[25] I do not want it implied that since this statement is made in a criticism of Davies' approach that the statement itself is discredited. It is a case of a

had been, Christ must be for Paul the new Torah. From this association naturally flow the references in Paul to the pre-existent and creative Christ.[26] In this rather tightly woven presentation Davies fails to ask certain basic questions: In what sense did the rabbis regard the Torah as pre-existent, and for what reason was this direction to the understanding of Torah given? Did Paul understand pre-existence in the same way and if so, in what particular circumstances? Was he moved to the category of pre-existence simply because it came in the "package" of implications relating to Torah and hence to Christ; or did the idea of pre-existence belong to the dimensions of concern about life and the universe felt by Paul and his readers, and hence provide a structure for an understanding of redemption? Did the rabbis, and Paul, always view pre-existence in the same way, that is, ideally or mythologically or philosophically?

In his handling of the matter of pre-existence, Davies thus is really unfair both to the rabbis and to Paul. In addition, he fails to explain why, if Christ's pre-existence was predicated upon Jewish assertions concerning the pre-existent Torah, the very Jewish wing of the church, the Ebionites, had no conception of Christ as pre-existent. Not all the

---

true statement used in an argument logically invalid. As to the centrality of Christ, I agree. As Eduard Schweizer put it: "Jesus Christ is the sole content of the Christian message. This is true in the most stringent sense. . . . To the primitive church Christology is the center of her message" (*Lordship and Discipleship*, trans. H. Van Daalen [Studies in Biblical Theology, No. 28; London: SCM Press, 1960], p. 94).

[26] *Paul and Rabbinic Judaism*, pp. 147 ff.

church felt the need for such Christology. Did the Ebionites, and the rabbis as well, deny the legitimacy of the whole concern about the nature of the human body and the physical universe, concerns that elsewhere prompted an array of myths about creation and pre-existence? As this could be handled by a reaffirmation of the Genesis creation accounts, what other reasons moved the rabbis to statements about pre-existence? These questions still remain at the close of Davies' discussion.

This brief survey of methods of interpreting Paul's Christology, methods that depend in varying degrees upon "definition by source," is designed solely to reveal the inadequacy of the approach, in spite of the value of each of these works as a source book of valuable collections of data and references. It is quite evident that it is not sufficient to ask of a passage that reflects the idea of pre-existence: What is its source? Even if the source were known, the same questions must be asked of the source that are asked of the text: What is the function of the idea of pre-existence within the context where it is found? How is pre-existence conceived in each particular affirmation?

It should be apparent at this point that the primary method to be employed here will be definition by function; that is, what each writer in each situation is intending to say by using the category of pre-existence. This will allow for openness to selection and creativity on the part of each writer studied; it will prevent leveling the Bible and destroying the variety in its affirmations; and it will enable us to move inside the material to a greater degree. The study itself will be the proof offered for the validity of the method.

Our procedure will be to look first at affirmations of pre-existence in background materials which are tributary to the New Testament. In no sense is this a chase after sources, but rather this survey will serve specific purposes spelled out at the beginning of chapter I. Chapter II will be an application of the method of investigation used in chapter I to the New Testament materials affirming the pre-existence of Christ. Having seen to what use the early church put the idea and with what modifications, we will then, in chapter III, raise the question of the meaningfulness of this category for our understanding of reality, in which not only Christ but we also participate. If it is concluded that pre-existence is no longer a meaningful way of affirming anything about Christ or about ourselves, is it because the category is out of date, or is it because what it affirms is not truth about life and reality? On the one hand, the problem may be one of language. Perhaps new categories and terms can affirm about Christ what the ancients expressed with pre-existence. On the other hand, there may be the far greater problem of understanding reality. Perhaps no understanding of the structure of reality satisfactory to contemporary man allows room for dimensions that transcend historical existence. The last chapter will conclude with suggested guidelines for a continued pursuit of the problem raised by this investigation of the meaning of the pre-existence of Christ.

(1)

Affirmations of Pre-existence in New Testament Background Materials

The purpose of this chapter is twofold: to establish by demonstration the validity of the method to be employed in examining New Testament affirmations of the pre-existence of Christ, and to provide an introduction to the general category of pre-existence in the religio-cultural milieu of the early church.

Briefly stated, the method of this study is the examination of ancient texts which contain expressions of the category of pre-existence in order to understand the functions of the category. This approach insists that an understanding of pre-existence will come through an investigation of the *functions* of this category for various writers rather than through the effort to locate *sources* of the category. Definitions by source, as was pointed out in the Introduction, have proved inadequate as a method of getting at the meaning of New Testament terms and concepts.

The expression "background materials" rather than the term "sources" has been deliberately employed here for several reasons. It was felt that the term "sources" would have implied that in the materials before us we have the original formulations of statements about pre-existence. In some cases this may be so; in others, these may have drawn upon sources even more remote. To prove or disprove this is not the present concern, for the function to which a statement is put may have guided the writer in selecting as well as formulating, in modifying as well as creating. The design is simply to point out that function is our best guide to understanding the statements *as they now stand*. In addition, the term "sources" would have implied that there was some direct connection between these materials and the New Testament passages to be considered in chapter II. That such relationships do exist in some cases has been proved to the satisfaction of some investigators but not of others.[1] Again, we here neither affirm nor deny the relationships between these materials and specific New Testament passages, as that is not necessary to the present purpose. Rather, we here deal only with the question of definition by function.

The canon by which the materials for this investigation were chosen was that they should represent a variety of formulations and uses of the idea of pre-existence. This survey of background materials will focus upon the following pre-

---

[1] An example of a rather judicious use of background materials without depending on "sources" to provide definitions of ideas is found in Reginald Fuller, *The Foundations of New Testament Christology* (New York: Scribner, 1965).

existent "beings" or entities: Sophia in the Jewish Wisdom literature; the Logos in Philo of Alexandria; the Son of Man in I Enoch; the Torah of the rabbis; the Logos of the Stoic philosophers; and the Redeemer myths of Gnostic religions.

Sophia of the Wisdom Literature.[2] In its common and perhaps earliest usage Wisdom was a description of a common-sense philosophy of life with a religious orientation. However, the figure of Wisdom came to acquire the qualities of a personified, even hypostatized, principle that existed before creation and was involved in the creative process. In Job 28, Wisdom underlies the order of the universe and the lives of men, but whether or not she is described as having an independent existence is not clear. However, in Proverbs 8, Wisdom is personified, given self-consciousness, and then involved in the creation at its beginning (8:22), as a master workman[3] beside God (8:30). In the apocryphal Ecclesiasticus, Wisdom is portrayed in the familiar image of a woman (ch. 15), and is the first of God's creation (1:4). Wisdom is universal (24:6), but she seeks a dwelling place among men (24:7). The Creator grants her a place in the tents of Jacob (24:8-12), where she takes the form of "the book of the covenant of the Most High God, the law which Moses commanded us" (24:23).

However, it is in the pseudo-Solomonic Wisdom of Solo-

---

[2] For our purposes here, the figure of Wisdom will be examined only as it appears in Job 28, Prov. 8, Ecclus., and Wis. of Sol.

[3] A variant reading is "a little child."

mon, dated 100-50 B.C., that the figure of Wisdom receives its highest development.[4] She is not only the guide of pious Jews (chs. 1-5, 10-12) whom to forsake is disastrous (chs. 13-19), but she herself is divine both in nature and function (chs. 6-9). She is an emanation from God (7:25), an associate in his work (8:4), and sits by his throne (9:4). She fashions, pervades, oversees, renews, performs, and manages all things (7:22-27; 8:1, 5). She not only existed before creation (9:9), but by her God created (9:1). In relation to God, Wisdom is the effulgence of light, the unspotted mirror of God's working, the image of God's goodness, the effluence of his glory, and the breath of his power (7:25-26).[5]

It is clear from these few references that the Wisdom figure appears at times to be a personification of God's mind or will, at other times to be a principle, and at other times to be hypostatically conceived; that is, as being separate from God and yet of the same substance.[6] In other words, the

---

[4] This is generally regarded to be true even if there is disagreement over the chronological order of Job 28, Prov. 8, Ecclus., and Wis. of Sol. Job 28 is regarded by some as a line of development separate from the others. Ecclus. is dated 200-180 B.C. and Wisdom, 100-50 B.C. Cf. W. L. Knox, "The Divine Wisdom," *JTS*, XXXVIII (1937), 230-37, and the introductory articles in R. H. Pfeiffer, *History of New Testament Times* (New York: Harper, 1949) and R. H. Charles, *Apocrypha and Pseudepigrapha of the Old Testament* (Oxford: Clarendon, 1913), Vol. I.

[5] On the problem of the integrity of the book, in addition to the above, cf. Addison Wright, "The Structure of Wisdom 11-19," *Catholic Bible Quarterly*, XXVII (1965), 28-34.

[6] For a discussion of hypostatization as a part of the process of concretization, cf. Helmar Ringgren, *Word and Wisdom* (Lund: Haken Ohlssons Bok-

language describing Wisdom is very similar to the language of the trinitarian formulas of the fourth century when the church sought to define the orthodox position with reference to the relation of the Son to the Father: one substance, two persons. At times the language is mythological, and the reader gets an image of a pre-existent being in the presence of God, a being called Sophia. In other passages the language is philosophical, and one can grasp only the description of a principle of Wisdom pervading the universe. As Helmar Ringgren has put it, "Wisdom has an obscure position between personal being and principle. She is both, and she is neither the one nor the other." [7]

This "obscure position" can best be understood in the light of the writer's purpose and the function of Sophia within that purpose.[8] Wisdom lore as it first appeared among the Hebrews was almost completely international, being in no way nationalized or integrated into the religion of Israel.[9] Wisdom was the summary of experience common to all peoples, distilled into proverbs and brief exhortations. He who followed those maxims had found "Wisdom." However,

---

tryckeri, 1947). W. J. Ferrar calls the language of chs. 6-9 poetic (*The Uncanonical Jewish Books* [London: SPCK, 1918], p. 37). A. T. S. Goodrick says the discussion is pure abstraction "with careless remarks to the contrary" (*The Book of Wisdom* [New York: Macmillan, 1913], p. 418). Note also O. S. Rankin, *Israel's Wisdom Literature* (Edinburg: T. & T. Clark, 1936), pp. 228 ff.

[7] *Word and Wisdom*, p. 119.

[8] Pfeiffer (*History of New Testament Times*, p. 325) accounts for this obscurity by questioning the integrity of the book. He says chs. 1-5 are to Jews, 6-19 to Gentiles.

[9] In the canonical Wisdom materials, only in Eccles. 1-2 are there even slight references to events in Israel's history.

in Ecclesiasticus and Wisdom of Solomon, internationalism and nationalism are both present, the vocabulary and doctrines of the Hellenistic culture being placed alongside the exaltation of Judaism with her heroes and institutions.[10] Wisdom is in all nature and is available to all men everywhere, and yet she is the peculiar possession of Israel.

The tensions between universality and particularity are not new to Israel, as the opposing theses of the books of Ruth and Esther illustrate; but in the Hellenistic period the outside pressures toward universalism are particularly attractive, with lofty philosophical systems, the extolling of virtues, and the love of learning. How can there be an honest recognition of the values and virtues and the evidences of God among all men without the loss of Israel's identity, peculiar heritage, and mission? How can Israel be firmly committed to her own particular tradition of faith and yet be open and tolerant toward other commendable views? As was Logos in the hands of Christian apologists, so here Sophia—preceding and permeating all creation, being with God and in just men everywhere, and yet, in a peculiar way, dwelling in the tents of Jacob—enables the writers to negotiate the international-

---

[10] Note especially Ecclus. 1:9; 15:14; 16:24-30; 24:3-6; also 10:4, 8; 10:19-22; 39:21 ff. for the universal themes in nature, in providence, in knowledge of God. And yet Israel is in a special class (17:17; 24; 36:1-10; 44:50). Also in Wis. of Sol. note the two themes of chs. 6-9 and 10-12. J. Reider refers to Menzel's list of 135 points of contact with Greek philosophy in *The Book of Wisdom* (New York: Harper, 1957), p. 31; e.g., the Stoic virtues (8:7), pre-existence of the soul (8:19), the body as a clay prison (9:15). Cf. also J. C. Rylaarsdam, *Revelation in Jewish Wisdom Literature* (Chicago: University of Chicago Press, 1946), pp. 40-41.

national, universal-particular tension. As J. A. F. Gregg has expressed it, Wisdom

co-ordinates Greek thought with Hebrew revelation and correlates (as functions of the same being) the various operations of creative activity, guidance of history, advancement of science and history, moral elevation of mankind, and mediation between God and man. He [the writer] hopes, while never passing the bounds of orthodoxy, to show that Judaism is not merely an insulated national creed but one standing in relation with truth wherever found.[11]

In the service of these ends, the writer makes use of Sophia, a precreational and transcreational personification and hypostasis of a divine attribute. The use of the terms and categories of Greek thought, however, are always subject to Judaism's monotheism, and the writer never quite crosses the line into dualism by postulating a second Eternal. The Wisdom figure is not allowed to threaten the basic creed of Israel: "The Lord thy God is *one.*"

What function does the category of pre-existence serve here? Sophia is the precreational wisdom of God, which thereby transcends all local or particular expressions of wisdom and yet which is available to all men, since Sophia left her stamp upon all that had been made. All intelligent men recognize the intelligibility of the universe. Over against this, however, Judaism understood her place among the nations as a peculiar and special one. This peculiarity and

---

[11] *The Wisdom of Solomon* (Cambridge: Cambridge University Press, 1922), p. xxiv.

particularity of Judaism was harmonized with the universal evidences of God by means of the Wisdom figure which, while conveyed to all men through creation, came to dwell in a special way in the tents of Jacob. Wisdom became "incarnate" in the book of the covenant.[12]

The Logos of Philo. Philo was a wealthy politicus in the Jewish sector of Alexandria about 25 B.C. until A.D. 50. Through preaching and writing he was a guide for Alexandrian Jews in the cultural and religious clash between Judaism and Hellenism. His works are related to the Wisdom literature, especially the Wisdom of Solomon, both chronologically and theologically, but in this background survey he is for several reasons considered separately.

First, Philo's affirmations of pre-existence primarily involve Logos or Word rather than Sophia,[13] and therefore in him we encounter another of the principal terms of the mythological and philosophical language of the Mediterranean and Near Eastern world. Second, he differs from the Wisdom writers not simply in terminology but in the degree of the adjustment or transformation of Judaism in his hands. For example, in Wisdom of Solomon 10-12, the heroes of Israel are reinterpreted to the extent that they remain throughout

---

[12] Ecclus. 24:8.

[13] But Philo uses Sophia also. Logos is the source of Sophia (*De Fuga* 97), yet elsewhere Sophia is mother of Logos (*De Fuga* 108). Logos flows from Sophia (*De Somn.* II, 242, 245), and yet the two are equated (*Leg. Alleg.* I, 19, 65). E. R. Goodenough regards the two terms interchangeable (*By Light, Light* [New Haven: Yale University Press, 1935], p. 23).

historical characters, concrete examples of Wisdom in men. The universal is subservient to the concrete. However, in Philo, Israel's characters, her customs, her institutions, and her history are treated as allegories of the inner drama of the soul. The concrete is subservient to the universal. Nothing destroys history with such subtle effectiveness as does allegory, in which the concrete is but an illustration of the universal and transcendent. Before proceeding farther, a look at Philo's context will help us understand the role of the pre-existent Logos in his thought.

The severest tests of Jewish particularity in Alexandria came not in the occasional pogroms, but in the everyday unconscious as well as conscious influences of Hellenism. Greek was the language of school, street, and even synagogue, and language carries more than superficial influences.[14] Not so attractive to the Jews were the cults of popular religion, but here the Jews often found company among the Greek philosophers who also denounced idolatry. Were the Jews, then, kin in a deeper sense to these nobler Greeks?

In this context Philo translated and reinterpreted Judaism, making it more palatable for Greek tastes.[15] In so doing it

---

[14] H. A. Wolfson's argument that Philo was Hellenized only on the level of language is therefore weak. See next footnote.

[15] The extent of the Hellenization is still debated. "The whole question of 'translation' not merely from one language to another but from one world of ideas to another is exceedingly complex" (Gregory Dix, *Jew and Greek* [New York: Harper, 1953], p. 80). The debate is perpetuated by the fact that Philo interpreted Judaism as philosophical mysticism, and yet he remained orthodox in his practice of all the customs. E. R. Goodenough, reading the interpretation, says that for Philo, Judaism was a mystery (*By Light, Light*, p. 7), and Wolfson, reading the practice, keeps Philo at one with the rabbis (*Philo* [Cam-

is evident he was under the influence of Plato's ideal world, Pythagorean subjectivism, and especially the Stoic Logos. In his hands, however, the Logos had a different and distinct function. Let us look briefly at Philo's use of the pre-existent Logos in its relation to God, to the universe, and to man.[16]

In relation to God, Logos is himself "theos" (*De Somniis* I, 229), existing before the world (*Legum Allegoriae* III, 175). Logos is not uncreated as God, and yet not created as human beings (*Quis Rerum Divinarum Heres* 42, 206). Logos is the man of God (*De Confusione Linguarum* 11, 41), the image of God (*De Confusione Linguarum* 28, 147), the mate of God (*De Specialibus Legibus* II, 31), the true and first begotten son (*De Agricultura Noë* 12, 51; *De Mutatione Nominum* 114-16). In relation to the world, Logos is the instrument by which God framed the world (*De Cherubim* 35, 127; *Legum Allegoriae* III, 31, 96) and is the image and character which was stamped upon the world (*De Somniis* II, 5, 45; *De Plantatione Noë* 19). In fact, the intelligible world which was the pattern for the visible is called Logos

---

bridge: Harvard University Press, 1947], I, 31 ff.). Wolfson's efforts are strained, but Goodenough seems too extreme the other way. W. L. Knox modifies Goodenough but is too philosophical, I feel (*St. Paul and the Church of the Gentiles*, p. x). My own position is nearer Bevan, who sees Philo as a Jew but one who is a religious preacher, interested in the religious experience, an experience best described as mystic. God is transcendent and the soul seeks to return to him. The nature of salvation and the means of attaining it are Hellenistic. ("Hellenistic Judaism," *The Legacy of Israel*, ed. E. R. Bevan and Charles Singer [Oxford: Clarendon, 1928], pp. 45-60.)

[16] This sketch is necessarily selective since there are over 1,300 references to Logos in Philo. All references here are from the Loeb Classical Library edition of Philo's works.

(*De Opificio Mundi* 25). Logos is captain and steersman in the management of the universe (*De Cherubim* 36). In relation to man, it must first be understood that there are two kinds of man, the heavenly and the earthly (*Legum Allegoriae* I, 31-32).[17] The heavenly is in God's image, has no corruptible parts, and is "true man," the Logos (*De Mutatione Nominum* 181). The earthly, having corruptible and irrational parts, is the work not only of the Logos but also of other powers (*De Fuga et Inventione* 13, 70). For this "mixed" man, imperfect, the Logos is God, but for the perfect, the primal God is God (*Legum Allegoriae* III, 207).

The function of Philo's affirmation of the pre-existence of Logos is not as diverse and confused as may here appear at first. Similarities with the figure of pre-existent Sophia are obvious, but Philo has done more than substitute Logos for Sophia. The pre-existent Logos here serves a different purpose for the writer. Philo is a mystic,[18] and it is better to understand him as allowing both Judaism and Hellenism to promote and inform the soul's quest than to debate whether his Judaism serves Hellenism, or vice versa. The true Israelite is the man who sees God. As a mystic, Philo holds God to be transcendent, the soul to be away from home until it is with God, and salvation to be this flight of the soul from the mundane world. But this implies something about this world and man's physical life that is not a part of the Genesis view of

---

[17] Philo so interpreted the two creation stories in Gen. 1-2.

[18] For example, note the pure mysticism in the soul's longing (*Quis R. D. Heres* 69, 40; *Leg. Alleg.* III, 44).

creation as the "good" work of the one God. The discontinuities between body and soul, man and the universe, are handled by the pre-existent Logos. As divine, the Logos is the explanation of the goodness, the "God-oriented" aspects of the life of man and the world; yet, as a being one step removed from the one primal God, the Logos is the explanation of the fact that there is distance between the ideal and the actual, the invisible and the visible, the heavenly and the earthly. This distance is thus explained in the theology of a mystic who cannot, on one hand, "soil" his image of God by involving him in the phenomenal world, but who, on the other hand, cannot depart from monotheism and account for the material world by having a second, lower-order, creator God.

While it is true, therefore, that Philo reflects some kind of marriage between Judaism and Hellenism, a union of Judaism's rites and Hellenism's interpretation, still it is not horizontally (Jew-Greek) that his pre-existent divine Logos has its primary function. In other words, Philo is not principally concerned with using a Logos doctrine to harmonize Jewish and Greek thought about God and the world. The Logos has its primary function, and hence is to be most properly understood, vertically (transcendent God–historical man), the dimension that for the mystic must be served by all other knowledge and experience.

The Logos as a precreational being of divine nature serves to explain the kinship to God of man and all creation. The Logos relates the contingent, relative, created order to the ultimate and unconditioned Absolute God. At the same time, the pre-existent Logos stands between God and creation as a reminder of the distance between the two. The distance is a gulf bordering upon dualism; a gulf between the essence of spiritual reality, the home of the soul, and the present existence in this world. The mystic, affirming both the distance and the kinship between the two realms, finds in the doctrine of a pre-existent Logos both the preserver of that distance and the bridge by which it may be spanned in the long homeward journey of the soul.

The Son of Man of I Enoch. With this section of the discussion we come to apocalyptic Judaism, which provides a view of pre-existence in the figure of the Son of Man. Since, however, a knowledge of the type of literature under consideration is vital to an understanding of the thought and purpose of its author, there is need here for a brief preliminary statement about apocalyptic literature and the circumstances out of which it arose.

The religion of Israel has been very much a religion of hope; "promise" and "fulfillment" are basic to it. However, her history reveals that very often Israel hoped against hope, and promise was apparently without fulfillment. The shape of Israel's earlier hopes (never fully abandoned) was national, and therefore very much related to soil, vineyards, flocks, and villages. However, when the horses and chariots of history had run repeatedly over hopes, these hopes, for some at least,[19]

---

[19] We do not know how widespread the apocalyptic form of the eschatologi-

took new shape. Seeing nothing of the promised future in the issues of the present and yet believing that God would keep his word, these seers envisioned the future breaking in upon the present. The injustices and incongruities of life were such that there seemed for this world no hope, only destruction. Therefore, the righteous would be rewarded and the evil punished in another age[20] when this age had passed away and there came a new heaven and a new earth,

> When the secrets of the righteous shall be
> revealed and the sinners judged,
> And the godless driven from the presence
> of the righteous and elect.[21]

Out of this combination of despair and optimism the apocalyptic literature arose. It was "created in an hour of desperate need, not in any self-conscious desire to set a fashion, but in eager desire to minister to the need." [22] The book of Enoch reflects such conditions: there is suffering at the hands of the unrighteous (94:6; 95:7; 96:7-8; 99:13), and some

---

cal hope was. However, any division of Judaism into distinct groupings, such as rabbinic, apocalyptic, mystic, etc., seems quite artificial. This point is well made by H. J. Schoeps (*Paul,* trans. Harold Knight [Philadelphia: Westminster, 1961], pp. 40-41).

[20] There were, of course, many forms of the apocalyptic hope, many combinations. For example, some forms combined national hopes and the apocalyptic with two judgments: a vindication of Israel with a millennium of peace, then a judgment of all nations according to righteousness.

[21] I Enoch 38:3. All references to Enoch will be from Charles, *Apocrypha and Pseudepigrapha,* Vol. II.

[22] H. H. Rowley, *The Relevance of the Apocalyptic* (London: Lutterworth, 1944), p. 13. It is significant that such a book appeared during a world war.

of the Jews are beginning to doubt the truth of God's justice and his promises (103:9-15). The writer seeks not only to encourage, but "to justify God's ways to man by making a sensible story of the whole course of history." [23]

It is not necessary to try to date precisely the work before us. From the time of Daniel (*ca.* 168-164 B.C.) to the collapse of the revolt of Bar Cochba (A.D. 135), the Jews were in a state of almost uninterrupted eschatological tension, and from this period came most Jewish apocalypses. It is apparently the case with Enoch that the work is composite, the various parts dating from different periods. Since our concern is with the statements pertaining to the Son of Man, attention will be focused upon the Similitudes (chs. 37-71), a section generally accepted by scholars as a literary unit distinct from the rest of the book,[24] and the primary source for these references.

The Similitudes are three: the first is a vision of the dwelling place for the Elect One and the elect ones, plus some initiation into astronomical secrets (37-44); the second is a vision of the Elect One, called Son of Man (46:1-3; 48:2-10) and Messiah (46:10), on his throne in righteousness, power, and judgment (45-57); the third is a vision of the bliss of the righteous, the punishment of the wicked (including wicked

---

[23] T. W. Manson, *The Son of Man in Daniel, Enoch, and the Gospels* (Reprint from "Bulletin of John Rylands Library," XXXIII [1950]), p. 186.

[24] Except for some older Noachic material in the Similitudes. For arguments as to date and integrity of this section of Enoch, cf. Charles, *Apocrypha and Pseudepigrapha*, pp. 168 ff.; Sigmund Mowinckel, *He That Cometh*, trans. G. W. Anderson (Nashville: Abingdon, 1956), pp. 354-55; E. Schürer, *A History of the Jewish People*, trans. S. Taylor and P. Christie (New York: Scribner, 1896), III, 2nd Div., 37-71.

angels), and the final translation of Enoch (58-71). Noticeable among the wicked are the kings and mighty of the earth (53:5; 62:1-12; 63). In this context, let us look at some of the statements about the pre-existent Son of Man.

> Because the Lord of Spirits hath chosen him [Son of Man],
> And whose lot hath the pre-eminence before the Lord of Spirits in uprightness for ever. (46:3*b*)

> Yea, before the sun and the signs were created,
> Before the stars of the heaven were made,
> His name was named before the Lord of Spirits. (48:3)

> And for this reason hath he been chosen and hidden before Him,
> Before the creation of the world and for evermore. (48:6)

> For from the beginning the Son of Man was hidden. (62:7)

Although in some of the descriptions the Son of Man is not active,[25] he does become involved in judgment and deliverance (45:3; 46:2; 69:26-29). His work is not only messianic in nature, but the Son of Man is called Messiah (46:10; 52:4), for obviously here the apocalyptic Messiah is expected to fulfill nationalistic hopes. [26] He is, of course, not a Messiah in the traditional "Son of David" sense of a human

---

[25] Manson, quite unhappy with the term "pre-existent," says the inactive pre-existent Son of Man might as well be nonexistent. Manson says the Son of Man is only a pre-existent idea (*Son of Man*, p. 186). More on this directly.

[26] E. Stauffer tries unsuccessfully to separate the Messiah and the Son of Man figure in Enoch ("Messias oder Menschsohn," *Novum Testamentum*, I [1956], 81-102).

deliverer; the nature of the hope upon which such messianism was structured is not here to be found. The times are too extreme and all hope lies beyond the contingencies of painful history. In fact, so extreme are the times that Wisdom, who in Ecclesiasticus had sought a dwelling place and found one in the tents of Jacob, here comes seeking a home, finds none, returns to heaven, and in her stead Unrighteousness comes, finding a welcome among men (42:1-3). Henceforth, wisdom is a secret, known only to the Son of Man and by him revealed to the elect (49:2-4; 61:5; 62:6).

In these dire circumstances, the description of the Deliverer can be expected to match in its loftiness the abysmal extremes of evil, and so it does. Fully adequate for the task is the Son of Man, premundane, supermundane, purely transcendent, and fully able to judge, deliver, and punish. It is true he has been hidden, and this hiddenness has seemed to the righteous as a delay, but this, too, is a part of the plan of God from the beginning.

If Daniel is this writer's source for the Son of Man figure, the figure has been reshaped for his purpose. Whereas in Daniel 7 the Son of Man is a symbol for the community of faithful Israel as over against the nations (pictured as beasts), here the Son of Man is with, but distinct and separate from, the elect ones. He stands not as the godly over against the ungodly, but in transcendence over both. Daniel's Son of Man has been transformed into a supermundane person, not a symbol for persons.[27]

---

[27] Clearly and concisely argued (with opponents noted) by Howard Teeple

In view of this imagery, vivid and in sharp focus, it is more in keeping with the writer's thought and purpose to say the Son of Man was pre-existent rather than predestined. As will be noted in the discussion of Torah immediately following, predestination is a category of the mind, an idea. That which is predestined is in God's mind or will, whereas pre-existence is a category that requires mythological language and individuation in imagery. This is precisely what we have in Enoch.[28] It would be a mistake to define pre-existence here as predestination simply by referring to the idea of pre-existence in the rabbis, as though the materials were parallel. It is true that in the rabbis pre-existence is primarily "ideal," in God's mind, and is therefore predestination.[29] It is also true that Enoch in his message of assurance to the saints is predestinarian, picturing the "not yet" as "already." But when Enoch asked about the Son of Man, "who he was and whence he was, and why he went with the Head of Days" (46:3), the answer is clear that he is pre-eminent forever, chosen and hidden before the world was created. It is not legitimate, therefore, to permit the few remarks of the rabbis concerning pre-existence (for reasons to be noted), couched in different literature and addressed to different problems, to sub-

---

in "The Origin of the Son of Man Christology," *JBL,* LXXIV (1965), 213-14.

[28] Supported by Charles, *Apocrypha and Pseudepigrapha;* G. H. Schodde, *The Book of Enoch* (Andover: W. F. Draper, 1882), pp. 47-48; E. K. T. Sjöberg, *Der Menschensohn im äthiopischen Henochbuch* (Lund: C. W. K. Gleerup, 1946), pp. 83 ff. Denied by Manson, *Son of Man,* pp. 181 ff.; H. L. Strack and P. Billerbeck, *Kommentar zum Neuen Testament aus Talmud und Midrash* (München: Beck, 1922-61), II, 334.

[29] See pp. 47-53 below.

due with heavy and undue caution this apocalyptic language.

The descriptions here are impressive and necessarily bold; their force and hence their function is lost when cramped into the category of pure "idea." "Ideas" are for calmer days. The historical circumstances in which Israel here lives are not such as to be a seedbed for hope; hope now must be grounded outside this present life, above historical contingencies. Despair, born of overwhelming evil and repeated suppressions of Israel's national dream, has moved in like a dense fog. For a savior to be effective he cannot be existent and historical; it is too late. He must be pre-existent and suprahistorical. Salvation lies with God's redeeming agent who cannot in any sense be hindered, limited, or dependent upon the vicissitudes of international politics. He is the pre-existent one, the Son of Man, supermundane, precreational. True, he has been hidden, but he is now to be revealed for the sake of Israel, and the Eternal will brake the wheels of time.

Quite clearly the writer's purpose, obviously different from that of Philo or the author of Wisdom of Solomon, has shaped the use of the idea of pre-existence to characterize the Redeemer[30] who stands outside and above creation and history.

The Torah of the Rabbis.[31] "Seven things were created

---

[30] For a discussion of the relation of the Enochian Son of Man to the Heavenly Man in other literature, cf. Carl Kraeling, *Anthropos and the Son of Man* (New York: Columbia University Press, 1927); R. M. Grant, *Gnosticism and Early Christianity* (rev. ed.; New York: Harper, 1966); Joachim Jeremias, "Anthropos," *ThWB*, I, 365-67. These works will provide extensive bibliographies.

[31] Torah here is taken to mean not simply "Law" (as in the Septuagint), but in the larger sense as the rabbis understood it: the whole of revelation. Cf.

before the world was created, these are they: the Torah, re-
pentance, the Garden of Eden, Gehenna, the Throne of Glory,
the Temple, and the name of the Messiah." [32] Again, "Be-
loved are Israel, for to them was given the desirable instrument with which the world was created . . . as it is said, 'For
I give you good doctrine; forsake ye not my Torah' (Prov.
4:2)." [33] Elsewhere, Torah is said to have existed one thousand years prior to creation,[34] and according to Rabbi Eliezer,
when God said, "Let us make man" (Gen. 1:26), he spoke
to Torah.[35] By the use of Prov. 3:19 some rabbis held that
the world was created for the sake of the Torah.[36]

Two facts are basic to our understanding the function of
this affirmation of the pre-existence of Torah. First, the idea
of pre-existence, and of a pre-existent Torah in particular,
was apparently not of prime importance among the rabbis.[37]
This is evident not only from the relatively few references,
but also from the fact that the idea never hardened into an

S. Schechter, *Some Aspects of Rabbinic Theology* (London: A. & C. Black,
1909), pp. 117-21.

[32] *Pesahim 54a,* trans. H. Freedman, in *Babylonian Talmud,* ed. I. Epstein
(London: Soncino, 1935-1952).

[33] A statement sometimes attributed to Rabbi Akiba and sometimes to Rabbi
Meir. Cf. *The Fathers According to Rabbi Nathan,* trans. Judah Goldin (New
Haven: Yale University Press, 1955), p. 162.

[34] The time varies in different traditions. Cf. "Torah," *The Jewish Encyclopedia,* XII, 197. Also *Legends of the Jews,* ed. Louis Ginzberg, trans. H. Szold
et al. (Philadelphia: Jewish Publishing Society of America, 1909-1939), V, 3-4,
n. 5.

[35] Cited by W. D. Davies, *Paul and Rabbinic Judaism,* p. 54.

[36] See references in G. F. Moore, *Judaism* (Cambridge: Harvard University
Press, 1927), I, 268. Discussion begins on p. 263.

[37] So agree most commentators. Cf. Ginzberg, *Legends,* V, 4, n. 5; 132-33, n. 2.
Also cf. G. F. Moore, *Judaism,* II, 344 ff.

article of faith normative for the community. The expressions, by the manner and occasion of their appearances seem more doxological than didactic, and the influence of the idea is to be found more in popular literature than in dogma.[38]

The reason for this apparent disinterest in pre-existence is evident when one begins to ask why there was such interest in pre-existence in the general milieu in which the rabbis lived. As will be noted later in this chapter, basic to much of the concern reflected in ancient cosmogonies and cosmologies was the conviction that man's basic problem is creatureliness, not sin. Man felt a sharp discontinuity existed between what truly *is* and what *came to be* with the appearance of the material world. This discontinuity between man's spirit and the material universe, between man's soul and his body, was the No. 1 problem posed to religion and philosophy. Answers that asserted creation itself was a "fall" or the work of a lesser god or demon were, of course, totally rejected by the rabbis as irreconcilable with the doctrine of creation. The fundamental belief in the goodness of creation as the gracious act of the one God discarded as illegitimate the concerns that produced doctrines of pre-existence, and to entertain such ideas, even when domesticated to Judaism, would have been to compromise. This is not to say that Judaism was totally immune to these anxieties usually associated with Gnosticism. On the contrary, there existed from ancient times circles of mysticism and apocalypticism within Judaism, both of which were efforts to escape, or be rescued from, an intolerable his-

---

[38] Schechter, *Some Aspects of Rabbinic Theology,* p. 130.

torical situation.[39] Mysticism sought to rise to the realm of *present* spiritual reality and apocalypticism was oriented toward the *future*, the end of all things. Neither perspective, therefore, showed great interest in pre-existent conditions, that is, in the state of spiritual realities before the beginning of history. And the rabbis preferred not to meet the anxieties about existence by developing their own complex of antemundane realities and pre-existent worlds of pure bliss, but by a reaffirmation of the doctrine of creation. God said, "It is good."

The second fact basic to our understanding of these references to the Torah is that, while not of prime importance, affirmations of pre-existence do clearly occur, as the quotations above testify. What is the function of these affirmations? As they stand in the texts cited, these references to a pre-existent Torah are too mild and too doxological to be viewed as debate with heretics.

Some commentators begin by saying that Torah was identified with the Wisdom figure as in Proverbs 8 and Job 28, and hence since Wisdom was described as pre-existent and the instrument of creation, so was Torah.[40] There is no question

---

[39] Varying degrees of modification of the positive attitude toward the universe and historical existence as represented by the Genesis account are to be found in apocalypticism, mysticism, and gnosticism. Apocalypticism has been noted above. For discussions of Jewish mysticism and gnosticism, cf. the writings of G. Scholem, esp. *Jewish Gnosticism, Merkabah Mysticism, and Talmudic Tradition* (New York: Jewish Theological Seminary of America, 1960). For a denial of any Jewish Gnosticism, cf. H. J. Schoeps, *Urgemeinde, Judenchristentum, Gnosis* (Tübingen: J. C. B. Mohr, 1956).

[40] Cf. Moore, *Judaism*, I, 265-68; V, n. 30; Davies, *Paul and Rabbinic*

but that by means of Prov. 8:22-30 this identification was made;[41] but to begin there is to begin in the middle of the story, for there had to be a reason for this identification. From the viewpoint of the rabbis that reason lay in the task of defining and solidifying postexilic Israel.

When the nation and the cultus no longer existed because of the exile and dispersion, Israel had to be redefined, and that redefinition came in terms of the Torah. It was the Torah that gave a new center of gravity, that created a community, and that gave Judaism its distinctive character. An Israelite was one who assumed the burden of the Law, and the most characteristic mark of Jewish piety was devotion to the Torah. While it is true that we possess no record that enables us to trace this process of absolutizing the Torah,[42] and with that process to note the beginnings of the synagogue, the Pharisees, and the scribes, yet that such occurred is marked in the extant literature. From the Old Testament, Ezra–Nehemiah, and Psalms 19 and 119 [43] testify to the centrality of Torah. In the Apocrypha, Tobit and Judith reflect a righteousness based on the Law; Ecclesiasticus (16:26–17:24;

Judaism, pp. 147 ff.; Schechter, *Some Aspects of Rabbinic Theology*, pp. 127 ff. This identification gave Torah its personification in certain passages.

[41] Strack-Billerbeck, *Kommentar zum NT*, II, 353-55.

[42] Concise discussions of what probably was happening can be found in G. H. Box, *Judaism in the Greek Period* (Clarendon Bible; Oxford: Clarendon, 1932), V, 73 ff.; W. O. E. Oesterley and T. H. Robinson, *Hebrew Religion* (New York: Macmillan, 1930), pp. 360 ff.; John Bright, *A History of Israel* (Philadelphia: Westminster, 1959), pp. 416 ff.

[43] Jacob Z. Lauterbach ("The Pharisees and Their Teachings," *Rabbinic Essays* [New York: University Publishers, 1951], p. 117) thinks these psalms were written by Pharisees or their predecessors.

19:20; 38:24) affirms Wisdom is embodied in the Torah; I Maccabees describes the Jewish revolt as stemming from violations of the Law and celebrates the fact that the army of Israel was true to that Law (1:11-15; 2:32-38). To this evidence may be added the New Testament with its representation of Torah-centered Judaism encountered by Jesus and Paul. As further evidence stands the Mishnah, the very existence of which is testimony to the exaltation and absolutizing of the Torah. Something of a climax in the process is represented both by the Book of Jubilees, which pushes the Law back into primeval times (chs. 2-6, 16, 21), and by the passages already quoted from the rabbis concerning the Torah's existence before the world was created.

The story of the absolutizing of Torah is the story of the victory of the Pharisees over the Sadducees. The Sadducees held the Law to be binding because of the oath taken to keep it. The Pharisees maintained that the Law was binding, but not because of the oath or the decision of an assembly or any other contingency. "This authoritative character was something inherent in the Torah itself. The Divine origin of the Torah was for them sufficient reason for man to obey it." [44] It was for all of life, for all men, for all time. It was the inevitable result of this process, and as a climax to it, that the affirmation of the pre-existence of the Torah is to be understood.

What, then, does pre-existence mean in this usage? It is almost a synonym for predestination in the sense that Torah

---

[44] *Ibid.*, p. 118.

has existed forever in the mind and will of God. The Torah is absolute, not contingent upon the vicissitudes of history nor the favor or disfavor of the community; Torah is the expressed will of the Eternal. It is not from man but from God; it is of divine origin; it is pre-existent.

The Logos of the Stoics. At no point in the study of Christology is there more need to bring to the materials a principle of interpretation, a canon for making judgments, than there is in the consideration of Logos; for with this one word the mind is deluged by Stoics, Philo, the Fourth Gospel, Gnostics, and the Christian apologists. In the preponderance of material, shades of meaning and differences between mythological and philosophical uses of the idea are often blurred, or do not appear at all. We are here concerned not with the history of the Logos idea but with its characteristic function[45] in the thought of the Stoics, with whom the Logos idea first became a distinctive element in a system of philosophy. If the method is valid here, it could then be taken to the other writers or schools to understand the meaning of Logos in the hands of each.

The average Greek of the fifth century B.C. had two main guides and sanctions for his conduct: the welfare of the inde-

---

[45] I use the word "characteristic" with caution, for Stoicism changed in the course of its history (300 B.C.–A.D. 200). Of the early Stoics (Zeno, Cleanthes, Chrysippus) we have only fragments. Most of our material is post-Poseidonius, from the Roman Stoics (Seneca, Epictetus, Marcus Aurelius). The fundamentals that are basic to our point, however, are found throughout.

pendent city of which he was a citizen and the religious and social traditions of his fathers. He had already loosened his hold upon these traditions due to the philosophers' ridicule of popular religion and superstition, but he still had his city. However, in the fourth century B.C., with the destruction of the city-state, the citizen of Greece had lost his address and with it his security and his identity.

When Zeno, considered to be the founder of Stoicism, arrived in Greece (*ca.* 320 B.C.), generals of the now deceased Alexander the Great were dividing the empire. All was in a state of flux and uncertainty, and it was in this political, social, religious, and psychological atmosphere that Stoicism took shape. In this light one understands Gilbert Murray's judgment: "Stoicism was primarily a religion for the oppressed, a religion of defense and defiance." [46] Religion is the proper word, for Stoicism was from its inception a religious philosophy.

Zeno found in Greece two emphases which he compounded into one: the Megarian school stressed the importance of the universal in understanding life and reality; the Cynics centered upon the individual, ridiculing the artificiality of universal concepts and of social structures. [47] The resultant Stoic concern was to bring unity to the life of the individual, but this could be done only by setting man in the context of a cosmos, an ordered world. "The one purpose [of Stoicism]

---

[46] *Stoic, Christian and Humanist* (New York: W. W. Norton, 1941), p. 91.
[47] For fuller discussion, cf. Edward Caird, *The Evolution of Theology in the Greek Philosophers* (Glasgow: J. MacLehose & Sons, 1904), II, 66 ff.

is to give unity to man's life, a unity which nothing can come from without to disturb. ... To give unity to the life of man, it is necessary to conceive the world of which he is a part as a unity." [48] As Marcus Aurelius was later to argue about cosmic order: "Think you that order subsisting within yourself is compatible with disorder in the All?" [49]

The early Stoics, therefore, would have none of the Platonic divisions between transcendent and immanent, between spirit and matter, since such dichotomies destroyed unity in the cosmos and hence security for the individual. They went back to the ancient Logos idea for the principle of unity in the cosmos. It was not, however, to the Logos of Thales and Parmenides that the Stoics returned, for with these ancients Logos was a means of relating the *gods* to the universe, and here the felt difficulty for the Stoics was to explain *man's* relation to the universe. The Logos doctrine fully developed only when severed from a doctrine of a transcendent God.[50] For this reason the idea is not a monument to an innate religiosity among the Greeks but to their noble manhood, for it was in an effort to explain man to himself that the Stoic doctrine of the Logos arose. It was, therefore, to Heraclitus

---

[48] *Ibid.*, p. 82.

[49] "Meditation IV," 27. Cited by W. L. Davidson, *The Stoic Creed* (Edinburgh: T. & T. Clark, 1907), p. 25. One sees immediately in the idea of disorder in the cosmos a theme common to much ancient literature, including Col. 1:15-20, which speaks of reconciling the All.

[50] For a study of the development of the Logos idea, see Max Heinze, *Die Lehre vom Logos in der griechischen Philosophie* (Oldenburg: F. Schmidt, 1872); Anathon Aall, *Der Logos* (Leipzig: O. R. Reisland, 1896); Hans Leisegang, "Logos," *Pauly-Wissowa-Kroll*, XIII, 1055-69; T. F. Glasson, "Heraclitus' Alleged Logos Doctrine," *JTS*, III (1952), 231-38.

that Stoicism looked; for his physics, built on the concept of the primitive fire, and his Logos, the immanent divine reason permeating all things, provided the key ideas for the monistic view of the world.[51] Fire and Logos were not to be distinguished as matter and spirit, for the early Stoics made no such division; the two were but passive and active substances in a universe viewed as a *monon*. Stoicism was, therefore, a materialistic view, and since this view included God, it was pantheistic.[52] There could be no transcendent order, no supernatural, for such divisions in the order of reality would serve only to threaten the one thing needful if the Greek citizen was again to have security: a unified, ordered cosmos which was the *All* of reality.

God, for the Stoic, was the *logos spermatikos*, the germinative principle of reason in the universe; and in the dynamic cycle of the invariable order of existence, all is from God to God, issuing, becoming, being reabsorbed. "You exist as but a part inherent in a greater whole. You will vanish into that which gave you being; or rather, you will be transmuted into the seminal and universal reason [*logos spermatikos*]." [53]

There was not with this conception, however, a loss of individual identity, for the Stoics also spoke of the *logoi spermatikoi* giving form to each part of the whole. Since Logos

---

[51] Davidson, *The Stoic Creed*, pp. 87 ff.

[52] "Zeno says that the whole universe forms the substance of God" (Diogenes Laërtius, *Fragment 163*, given in E. Bevan, *Later Greek Religion* [Boston: Beacon, 1950], p. 1).

[53] Marcus Aurelius, "Meditation IV," 14. Note also his famous expression, "O Nature, from thee, in thee, unto thee are all things" (IV, 23).

was in all things, including man (*koinos logos*), the Stoic ethic was to live according to this reason, or according to nature. Physics provided the scaffolding for ethics,[54] and the noble life was based on *homologia*, self-consistency. Hence, this permeating Logos could be called *Nomos*, the norm or constitution for man and for society, its universality creating, in principle at least, a brotherhood of all humanity. Thus Cleanthes could sing:

> O sovran King . . .
> Thou dost direct
> The Universal Reason [*koinon logon*] which commixt
> With all the greater and lesser lights
> Moves through the universe. . . .
> Thou has fitted things
> Together, good and evil, that there reigns
> One everlasting Reason [*logos*] in them all.[55]

Is there in this system, then, an affirmation of pre-existence? Two facts stand out clearly even in this brief résumé. First, Stoicism knew no Logos distinct and separate from God.[56] Its strict monism did not permit even that degree of dualism. It was not until Stoicism was wedded to Platonism by Poseidonius and others that the Logos was viewed as having

---

[54] *The Hymn of Cleanthes*, trans. E. H. Blakeney (London: SPCK, 1921), p. 3.

[55] *Ibid.*, pp. 6-7.

[56] The only "separate" Logos they knew was this: Logos dwelt within a man as thought (*endiathetos*); when he spoke, he formed words from his thoughts; the Logos was then *prophorikos*. This distinction came into prominence in the Christian apologists in explaining the relation of the Logos-Christ to the Father.

distinct being, mediating between God and the world, as was noticed in Philo. Secondly, and this fact is implied in the first, this physical-ethical understanding of reality does not have a place for the idea of pre-existence because pre-existence implies separateness from, being apart from, by reason of priority of time or space. Stoic monism had as its purpose the creation of a sense of unity and a feeling of belonging for men who were without the old grounds of security. Any existence outside that unity, as pre-existence implies, would be a threat to it, a witness to a flaw in the system. The Stoic Logos, therefore, is "dia-existent," permeating, as a philosophical principle; not pre-existent, as a mythological being. Interestingly enough, there is, from some points of view, common ground here between the Stoics and the rabbis: neither possessed a world view that would breed ideas of pre-existence. For both, man was at home in the universe: for the rabbis, because of their doctrine of creation; for the Stoics, because of their doctrine of the Logos.

This leads us to observe, in anticipation of subsequent analyses of New Testament passages that speak of Christ in terms of the pre-existent Word (Logos) of God, that the immediate background for such passages could not be the Logos doctrine of the Stoics. For them there could be no pre-existent Logos calling the cosmos into being. No creator or agent of creation stood outside the cosmos because the cosmos was for Stoics the sum total of reality.

Myths of the Gnostics. Again, the sole concern here is to observe the functional nature of affirmations of pre-existence in a body of literature. This reminder is especially appropriate at this point where we approach an area so filled with questions for the investigators, questions that arise not only out of the confusedly syncretistic nature of Gnosticism itself,[57] but also out of the nature and dates of the sources.[58] However, since we are not here concerned to establish lines of relationships with New Testament affirmations, dates and evidences of dependence are not germane to this investigation. It will be necessary here to be selective both in the choice of materials and in the aspects of those materials to be discussed. The procedure will be to discuss briefly the conditions that bred and nurtured Gnosticism, the concerns which are reflected in its literature and the Gnostic response to those concerns, and then to look at statements of pre-existence in three different Gnostic systems. The three selected—Justin's Baruch, the system of Basilides, and Poimandres—represent

---

[57] Cf. G. Quispel, *Gnosis als Weltreligion* (Zürich: Origo Verlag, 1951); Kendrick Grobel, *The Gospel of Truth* (Nashville: Abingdon, 1960), pp. 12 ff.; Bultmann, *Primitive Christianity*, trans. R. H. Fuller (New York: Meridian, 1956), pp. 162 ff. This syncretism has made particularly difficult the problem of origins and whether or not Gnosticism had a redeemed redeemer before it was influenced by Christianity. On the present state of the problem of the redeemed redeemer, cf. J. M. Robinson's review of C. Colpe's *Die religionsgeschichtliche Schule* in *JBL*, LXXXI (1962), 287-89. Fruitful recent discussions as to the origins of Gnosticism have looked in the direction of heterodox Judaism; cf. R. M. Grant, *Gnosticism and Early Christianity*.

[58] Until modern times we were dependent upon the enemies of Gnostics for our information, primarily Justin, Irenaeus, Hippolytus, and Epiphanius. Since the Nag-Hammadi finds in 1945, many new materials are available. R. M. Grant (*Gnosticism* [New York: Harper, 1961]) has an anthology of sources from the new discoveries as well as the Christian apologists. The sources date from the second century A.D. and later, but the existence of pre-Christian Gnosticism is widely accepted.

three different accents upon the common theme of pre-existence.

The age of syncretism, of which Gnosticism was not only an expression but also the characteristic spirit, can be traced to the cultural and religious processes which followed the political uprooting basic to Alexander the Great's crusade. Alexander's vision was of one world; that vision was his message, and his armies were persuasive missionaries. The protecting walls of city-states and autonomous governments crumbled, and local deities which had cast comforting shadows over hearth and home toppled. The commitments that give men a sense of security are always particular, not general, and especially was this true in the East, where even the religions were particularized and concretized in ritual and myth. But the Greek capacity for abstraction came to the East and, without intending it, provided the wings whereby the East could move to the West. Into the wider circles of thought went hitherto unknown or little known cults and beliefs, blending, changing, forming new amalgams as men look to religion and its promises of salvation. From Phrygia came Cybele and Attis; Isis and Serapis came from Alexandria, Baal from Syria, Mithra from Persia, and, of course, Jehovah from Palestine. The Hellenistic culture became primarily religious, and the spiritual climate had three distinctive qualities: a concern for salvation, belief in a transcendent God, and an anticosmical dualism.[59]

---

[59] Hans Jonas, *Gnosis und spätantiker Geist* (2nd ed.; Göttingen: Vandenhoeck & Ruprecht, 1954), I, 74-80. The modified English translation (by

In this period when there was a general turning from the pages of history to the revelations of esoteric cults for a sure word about the future, the dominating force shaping creed and cultus was astrology. Centuries earlier, philosophers of Greece had pointed to the starry heavens for illustrations of order and harmony in the universe, but now it was with anxious eye that man scanned the heavens. The four basic elements of the universe, the *stoicheia,* identified by the Greeks with the constellations, came to be synonymous with the demonic powers believed to have their dwelling among the planets. The universe was seen as a hierarchy of powers: the sphere of the fixed stars, the seven spheres of the planets, and the sublunar region.[60] In their unalterable courses the stars ground out the destinies of men, and blind fate, *Heimarmene,* ruled supreme.[61] The experience of evil was not simply a moral question, but a characteristic of total existence.

For this ancient man the basic problem was existence itself, and from the platform of self-transcendence he viewed his problem, aware of that "something" within himself which refused to be confined to the narrow parentheses of time and place. Man, he thought, is soul in clay, eternity in time, a prisoner in an alien and hostile world. True possession of life, it was believed, would come with knowledge of its origin and nature, for it was ignorance and forgetfulness of life's origin

---

Jonas) of this volume is *The Gnostic Religion* (Boston: Beacon, 1958). Cf. pp. 31 ff.

[60] Franz Cumont, *Astrology and Religion Among the Greeks and Romans* (New York: G. P. Putnam's Sons, 1912), pp. 121-23.

[61] Schweizer, *Lordship and Discipleship,* p. 104.

and nature that made this life torment. "This not-knowing-the-Father became an anguish and a terror; and the anguish condensed like a fog so that none could see." [62] The Gnostic systems were attempts to guarantee this knowledge, and hence salvation, to those able to receive it. "What liberates is the knowledge of who we were, what we became, where we were, whereinto we have been thrown; whereto we speed, wherefrom we are redeemed; what birth is, and what rebirth." [63]

The reader can anticipate, therefore, finding in the Gnostic materials myths about the origin of the universe and of mankind and dramas of pre-existent persons in a supranatural world, of which "the drama of man in the natural world is but the distant echo." [64] However, it can also be expected that in each case the affirmation of *pre*-existence will be suited to the writer's own understanding of the basic problem of *existence*.

(1) Baruch is the name given to a document and to its principal character by the author, a late-second-century Gnostic named Justin.[65] Baruch is the bearer of the news of

---

[62] Grobel, *The Gospel of Truth* 17:10-13, pp. 40-42.

[63] *Excerpt from Theodotus*, 78:2. Here translated by Jonas in *The Gnostic Religion*, p. 45.

[64] Jonas, *The Gnostic Religion*, p. xiii.

[65] Apart from Hippolytus (*Refutation of All Heresies*, V, 23-27) we know nothing of Justin. This is strange in view of Hippolytus' description of him as the worst of all heretics and writer of many volumes. We may wonder how well Justin is represented by this one source. Hippolytus put Justin before Simon Magus in his discussion, but he is probably to be dated late second century. His system is much like that of the Ophites. Two recent treatments of Baruch are E. Haenchen, "Das Buch Baruch," *ZTK*, I (1953), 123-58, and R. M. Grant, "Gnosis Revisited," *Church History*, XXIII (1954), 36-45.

salvation. The writing is brief and obscure, and yet it properly represents Gnosticism at the point of our present concern, pre-existence. Gnostic systems were much concerned about origins and the pre-existent realm, for it is in this realm that the Gnostics found the meaning of life's whence, and therefore life's whither.

The book of Baruch affirms the pre-existence (before the creation of the universe) of three unbegotten principles, two male and one female. The supreme male principle is called the Good One (Luke 18:19), and he is transcendent, invisible, and in possession of foreknowledge. He is not directly involved in creation although he is said to be the ultimate cause, for before creation the Good One created the ideal pattern for all things. The second male principle is Elohim; also called Father of all begotten beings; invisible, without foreknowledge, but with knowledge (with some deficiency). The female principle is Edem or Israel, passionate, wrathful, double-minded, and double-bodied, half virgin and half serpent. Elohim and Edem desire each other, and of their union come twelve paternal angels, complimented with names such as Michael, Amen, and Baruch, and twelve maternal angels, given names that prophesy of their natures, names such as Babel, Achamoth, Naas, Satan, and Beliar. Together the twenty-four are called Paradise and are referred to allegorically as trees. Baruch is the tree of life; his counterpart among the maternal angels is Naas (serpent), the tree of good and evil. The paternal angels make man of the upper portions of the earth (Edem) and the beasts of the lower portions. Elohim imparts to man "spirit," and Edem gives him a "soul"; likewise Eve is made, the two existing as a memorial of the blissful union of Elohim and Edem. Edem's twelve angels form the four rivers of the garden (four seasons), and as they alternately rule, there is famine, disease, and illness on the earth.

When all has been formed, Elohim and his angels ascend to see if all is in good order, and while ascended, view the bright light of the Good One, and Elohim desires to enter his presence. With the Good One's permission he does so, without his angels. Elohim wants now to destroy the world in order to get back his spirit which was bestowed on man, but the Good One prevents it. Creation is left with Edem, who tries to lure Elohim back, and when she cannot, she sends Babel to cause divorce and fornication on the earth in order to bring anguish to Elohim's spirit in men. Naas seduces Edem and has unnatural relations with Adam.

To redeem man in whom his spirit resides, Father Elohim sends Baruch to call men to ascend to the Good One. Baruch goes to Moses, the prophets, and to the Gentile prophet Heracles, but in each case Naas frustrates his work. Spirit and soul struggle for control of man. Finally Baruch is sent to Jesus, son of Joseph and Mary, who succeeds in resisting Naas. Naas, in anger, has Jesus crucified. Jesus leaves his body to his mother Edem and commends his spirit to Father Elohim, and in his success Jesus is able to preach and teach this word about the Good One and the ascent to him. Those who are spiritual can hear and receive this word of Jesus, and they take a vow never to turn from the Good One to the earth and to creation.

Baruch obviously consists of a compound of elements from

the New Testament (I Cor. 2:9 and Paul's antitheses in Romans and Galatians), the Old Testament and Apocrypha (especially Genesis and the names of angels in the Apocrypha), and an old Greek cosmogonic myth.[66] But it is more than a compound; it has a shape and function in the writer's purpose.

While the book reflects many typically Gnostic themes (the transcendence of the Good One, the inferiority of Moses and the prophets, the dual nature of man, the cause of illness and disease, and a negative view toward the material creation), it is evident that Justin sees the primary problem of existence in terms of the love of man and woman. His system is not structured to wrestle with a Christological problem; Jesus succeeds against Naas, but he is only the son of Joseph and Mary, not the incarnation of a pre-existent one. Justin wrestles, rather, with the tension between Eros and Agape. He is careful to remove the Good One from the struggle, and yet he is unwilling to have a sharp dualism that regards matter as evil, woman as evil, and celibacy as the only good life. Matter is not evil and neither is marriage. The command to multiply and replenish the earth is good, but when this command is violated by Elohim's ascent from Eros to Agape, turning from his spouse to the higher love of the Good, there breaks out all manner of sexual misbehavior on earth. The evil on earth is not because of creatureliness. The Good One forbids Elohim's destroying the earth because nothing which has its ultimate source in the Good One could be essentially

---

[66] See Grant, "Gnosis Revisited," for references to this myth.

evil. Evil arises out of an apparently insoluble tension and frustration. Evil began as a result of Elohim's rising to the Good, his preference for God over, and to the rejection of, his wife. Justin's gospel, with all its unanswered implications, is a call for man to ascend to the Good One, listening to his own spirit and turning a deaf ear to his psyche and all earthly loves.

Justin's theology externalizes a problem that is internal, deep, and very real. Justin's affirmation of pre-existence, therefore, is focused upon this problem. Male and female principles existed before the universe and so are here to stay, a part of reality. Here is a function of the idea of pre-existence quite different from uses previously noted. Instead of looking to the realm of pre-existence for hope, Justin almost pessimistically concludes that the basic conflict of Agape and Eros, love of God and love of mate, is not a conflict the source of which lies in existence, but rather belongs to the very nature of reality, to the essence. This is what he means by positing male and female principles in the nature of reality; that is, by saying they are pre-existent. Man is not redeemed from his conflict of loves by death because this conflict is not confined to historical existence. Redemption comes when one knows the source and nature of this conflict and then, aware of the price involved, proceeds in full courage to ascend to the Good One who is perfect, remote, and unfrustrated.

(2) The system of Basilides,[67] a Gnostic leader who lived

---

[67] We will here draw upon Hippolytus' *Refutation of all Heresies* (VII, 20-27), which is generally regarded as more likely a report of Basilides' own system

in the first half of the second century, offers an entirely different framing of the idea of pre-existence. Yet here again we can anticipate that the description of the pre-existent state will be a characterization of life's "essence" apart from the drab and tragic trappings of existence.

There was a time (neither "was" nor "time" is to be taken seriously but are necessary for making the sentence) when there was altogether nothing. The nonexistent God, to be conceived only in terms of pure negation, willed to create a world. Here again, "willed" is not to imply volition, need, or sensibility, nor is "world" to be conceived in terms of any dimensions but rather is to be understood as a germ or seed that carries in itself a variety of forms and substances. The nonexistent God speaks and it is so. The doctrine of creation *ex nihilo* is not extreme enough to convey the thought here, for the nonexistent God created a nonexistent world out of nonexistent substance.

The germ or seed contains a threefold Sonship, one part

---

than is the more mythical system reported by Irenaeus (*Adversus haereses* I, 24). F. J. A. Hort considers Irenaeus' report to be referring to Basilides' disciples *ca.* fifty years later. Basilides himself is usually placed in Hadrian's time (A.D. 117-38) ("Basilides," *Dictionary of Christian Biography*, ed. William Smith and Henry Wace [Boston: Little, Brown, & Co., 1877] I, 268-81). For a discussion of the Basilidians of Irenaeus, cf. R. M. Grant, "Gnostic Origins and the Basilidians of Irenaeus," *Vigiliae Christianae*, XIII (1959), 121-25. Cf. also G. Quispel, "L'homme gnostique (La doctrine de Basilide)," *Eranos-Jahrbuch*, XVI (1948), 89-139; J. H. Waszink, "Basilides," *Reallexikon für Antike und Christentum*, I (1950), 1217-25. Other ancient sources for Basilides' system are Clement of Alexandria, *Strōmateis* III; VII; Tertullian, *De praescriptione* XLVI; Epiphanius, *Haereses* XXIV; Eusebius, *Historia ecclesiastica* IV, 7; Philaster, *Diversarum haereseōn liber* XXXII.

subtle, one part gross (opaque), and one part in need of purification. The first part, extremely refined and of one substance with the Father, flies upward and unites with the nonexistent God. The second part, unable due to its grossness to
bear itself aloft, is borne by the wings of the Holy Spirit; but
because it is lacking in some degree the qualities of the first
part of the Sonship, it does not attain to the same station with
the Father. The third part of the Sonship, which requires
purification, remains in the formlessness of the conglomera-
tion of the seed, its fate to be noted shortly.

After the first and second parts of the Sonship have ascended, the firmament is formed which separates the supra-
mundane from the mundane world. In the region of the lower
side of the firmament the seed bursts forth, and out comes
the Great Archon, head of the world. Rising to the firmament
and thinking it to be the ultimate end, the high than which
there is no higher, the Great Archon regards himself supreme
and begins creation. His first act is to create a son who is
superior to himself and who aids in the creation of the cosmos.
These dwell in the Ogdoad (Eighth Sphere above the earth).
Then from the seed comes another Archon who also creates a
son and they create this world. They dwell in the Hebdomad
(Seventh Sphere). The Archon of the Hebdomad is fabricator
of all subordinate things, and he it was who spoke to Moses
and the prophets. Notice here the typically Gnostic rejection
of this creation and the view of its creator as inferior to the
Supreme Father God. This lesser God, for the Gnostics, is the
God of Genesis 1-2.

At this point Basilides introduces the Gospel. The Gospel

comes down from the first Sonship in the presence of the non-existent God through the Holy Spirit to the Ogdoad, where the son of the Great Archon receives it. The son delivers it to the Great Archon who, upon learning that he is not the one supreme God, repents and is converted. On down to the Hebdomad the Gospel goes, converting the Archon. All the 365 angels and powers hear the Gospel. From here the light of the Gospel comes upon Jesus, and he is overshadowed by the power of the Most High. Jesus ascends, properly refined to take his place in the region of the first Sonship. There follow him upward all the souls of the third part of the Sonship which have remained in the conglomerate of formlessness. When all those who are able to receive the Gospel (here Gospel means knowledge of the nonexistent God, the Holy Spirit, and the first two parts of the Sonship beyond the firmament) have ascended, then the nonexistent God sends upon all the region below the firmament—that is, the Ogdoad, the Hebdomad, and the formlessness of the seed—a stupor so that those who are to remain forever in this region will have no desire for salvation. These are consigned to a blissful ignorance of life's ultimate source and meaning. It was part of the work of Jesus to fix and to confirm the bounds and orders of being, for when he died, he left behind that part of himself that belonged to each of the levels of being from the lowest to the highest before entering nonexistence; that is, on his upward flight, at each stage he shed that which belonged to the Hebdomad, to the Ogdoad, and to the Holy Spirit. Henceforth except for those souls in men able to receive the Gospel, nothing shall move from its fixed place. All this, including Jesus, was conceived in the mind of the non-existent God before the existence of the universe.

In spite of the philosophical rather than simply mythological dress, the distinguishing marks of Gnosticism are evident: the transcendent God aloof from the world; the subordinate Demiurge responsible for this world; the distinctions of physical, psychical, and spiritual modes of being; the predestined spiritual ones; the principalities and powers of the cosmos; and the ascent of Jesus, leading past the subfirmament regions into glory the souls of those receiving the Gospel of knowledge. It is possible to detect in the system materials from both biblical Testaments, from Plato, from Aristotle's orders of being, and possibly from the Buddhist emphasis upon the ultimate goal of nonexistence.[68] But our present concern is to ascertain what feature, what aspect, of this eclectic philosophy is paramount in the author's purpose, in the pursuit of which he employs an affirmation of pre-existence.

The simpler and sharper dualisms of other Gnostic systems are absent here, but not because this language is more philosophical; the reason is that Basilides does not see in them the primary problem of man. He gives no attention to the male-female problem, and he does not focus upon the spirit-matter, Jewish-Christian, divine-human (in Jesus) tensions as matters of prime importance. Apparently for Basilides the principal problem is existence itself, and redemption would not be exis-

---

[68] Cf. the article by H. A. A. Kennedy, "Buddhist Gnosticism, the System of Basilides," *Journal of the Royal Asiatic Society* (1902), pp. 377-415.

tence in a "fairer realm than this," but rather nonexistence. The highest compliment he can pay to God, the only way really to mark God's distance from us, is to speak of him as nonexistent. Beginning then with nonexistence as the highest order of being, Basilides explains how there came to be the lower orders of refined being, opaque or gross being, the firmament of spirit, the cosmos, the world, and the physical formlessness. Man is caught in these lower orders, but the elect ones know through the experience of Jesus that they can leave the physical, the psychical, and the spiritual behind in the ascent, coming finally to the bliss of nonexistence. The horrible fate that falls upon all other existent beings is the stupor that causes them to think that the present existence is ultimate. These tragic creatures live in, by, and for this world.

Basilides affirms, therefore, that that which pre-exists is nothing, nonexistence. He does say that the process he describes in his system was conceived in the mind of the nonexistent God, but he is not in any way elevating any aspect or dimension of existence to the status of pre-existence. Before existence there was nonexistence, and to nonexistence all the Sonship returns. All else is doomed, fixed in its own order of existence. To live forever would be hell; to cease to exist would be heaven.

(3) Poimandres[69] is the name of the first tractate in a

---

[69] I recognize the lack of a generally accepted definition of what is "Gnostic." I use Poimandres here to illustrate a perspective on pre-existence

collection of Hellenistic religious and philosophical writings called *Hermetica* after Hermes, the messenger of the gods.[70] Very likely the ideas presented in this literature are much older than the document itself, even though there is much disagreement among scholars as to the specific thought-world out of which the material came.[71]

The tractate opens with a description of a visionary situation in which the seer, in a kind of sleep, is visited by Poimandres, a being of great magnitude who is the mind of the Sovereignty. In reply to the seer's request to know of the origins of things, and of God, Poimandres presents a vision of the beginning of creation, but soon the vision is replaced by a descriptive account.

The vision of the cosmogony (pars. 4-11) begins with pure Light, out of a portion of which comes darkness, then

---

realizing that some would not classify it as Gnostic material. For example, R. M. Grant (*Gnosticism and Early Christianity*, p. 148) calls it "gnosticizing" or "semi-gnostic."

[70] I will here deal only with this first tractate, a work complete in itself and the most important (for our purpose) of the tractates. The authoritative text is that of A. D. Nock and A. J. Festugière, *Corpus Hermeticum* (Paris: Societé d'edition "Les belles lettres," 1945), Tome I, Traité I. As to the date of the material there is no certainty. W. Scott (*Hermetica* [London: Clarendon, 1924], I, 8-10) says before the fourth Christian century. C. H. Dodd (*The Bible and the Greeks* [London: Hodder & Stoughton, 1935], p. 209) says early second Christian century. R. Reitzenstein (*Poimandres* [Leipzig: B. G. Teubner, 1904], p. 36) puts the original form before the beginning of the second Christian century.

[71] Poimandres, unlike most of the tractates, is definitely familiar with Genesis and Adam, but Christianity is not reflected either in favorable or unfavorable light. As to the thought context for Poimandres, Reitzenstein discusses it in relation to Egypt and Iran; W. Scott sees primarily Greek influences; Dodd analyzes it in relation to Hellenistic Judaism.

smoke. With a lament and an inarticulate cry these change into a moist substance. From the Light, which is Mind, comes a Word (Logos), son of Mind, which stands upon the moist substance. Now in fixed gaze the seer beholds in the Light numberless Powers, and there appears the invisible ideal world, limitless archetype of the universe. The visible world is created by the Word according to this form. Of the four basic elements, earth and water move downward while fire and air, the pure and active substances, move upward. The First Mind, bisexual, gives birth to a second mind who is the Demiurge. This Demiurge makes from fire and air seven planets called Administrators who orbit the sensible world and who rule as Fate. From below in the earth and water, the Word beholds the Demiurge as one like himself, and so he flies upward and they are united. Now devoid of the Word (reason), earth and water (nature) produce subrational creation. Apparently this creative process is effected through the Administrators now circling in the heavens.

At this point (pars. 12-19) Poimandres tells of the creation of Man. The First Mind gives birth to Man, Primal Man in heaven, who is in the image of his father. First Mind, the Father, loves him and sets him over all that has been made. When Man sees what his brother, the Demiurge, has made, he wants to create also, and with permission moves into the sphere of the seven Administrators. Each of these seven gives Man some of his own nature as Man descends. When Man breaks through the spheres and sees his image reflected in Nature, he loves it, descends, and dwells with subrational Nature, who enfolds him in love. Thus it is that Man is twofold, immortal and mortal, above the spheres yet slave of Fate, sleepless yet oblivious, bisexual yet with carnal desire. Nature and Man produce seven bisexual humans with earth as the female element, water as the male, and the spirit from the region of fire and air. These are like Man and yet have mortal parts. After a period of time all creatures cease to be bisexual, are divided into two sexes, and are commanded to multiply.

Paragraphs 20-23 are devoted to a description of the two types of conduct among men. Those who know themselves to be immortal are pure, holy, and good. These have the protecting presence of Poimandres, who wards off carnal temptation, and ultimately they return to the Father, the Good. Those who set affections on the body wander in the darkness of the sense-world with inflamed desires and are subject to death.

The ascent of those who know themselves to be immortal and who have thus loathed the bodily senses takes place in this way (pars. 24-26): at the dissolution of the body the bodily senses return to the universe. At each of the seven spheres a clinging vice (lust, arrogance, falsehood, etc.) is left behind, and the spirit joins the Powers, praises the Father, and enters into God. This is the Good, the consummation, the goal of life.

Poimandres charges the seer to go preach, and the remainder of the tractate is an expression of praise to God and a description of the seer preaching the true knowledge of man's nature to those drunken, ignorant, and in error as to their true nature.

In addition to Genesis, the writer reflects an acceptance of

Platonic and Stoic ideas. His primary aim is clearly religious, not a philosophical quest of truth for its own sake. While the usual Gnostic patterns of dualism appear and the discontinuity between man and earthly existence is put in focus, there are elements that soften the sharp antitheses of some systems. Darkness is not present from the beginning; the Father God, while not the Demiurge, is involved with deliberation in creation; Man does not descend out of love for sensual nature; true knowledge is a gospel for any who will hear, not for just a chosen few; and moral conduct is the true reflection of whether a man has this knowledge.

What, then, is the writer's central message? There is no question but that his primary concern is to tell the truth about man's real nature and to have that truth propagated. The cosmogony is presented not as a matter of interest in itself but as a background for understanding man. It is important to notice that Primal Man did not pre-exist in the sense of precreation. There were three beings from the Father: Word, Demiurge Mind, and Primal Man; but only Word and Demiurge are precreational and are involved in creating the universe. Primal Man appears after the universe has been created, and although he asks to share in creation, he does not, apparently because it is already done. The involvement of Word and Demiurge in creation is planned, but not so with Primal Man. The Father's indulgent love, the catering to Primal Man by the Powers, and curiosity joined with an error in judgment contribute to his unplanned and tragic involvement in the world. But in the process of this heavenly Man becoming earthly man, he never loses his otherness, that ontological difference between himself and nature. Something of Man, the image of the Father, remains in fallen man.

The writer, therefore, affirms pre-existence as precreation in his explanation of how the universe came to be, but only as the context of man's plight. As far as man is concerned, pre-existence is not precreation but pre-earthly life, prehistory, preinvolvement in matter; Primal Man, not historical man, is the characterization of the real nature of man. It is this truth that man must know, and by knowing it, deny all carnal appetite and claim that status again. This myth of prehistorical existence declares that "at his center, man is above the promptings and necessities of nature." [72]

Conclusions. In all these selections of material containing affirmations of pre-existence, the texts themselves have been the primary witnesses to the meaning or meanings of pre-existence. We have examined briefly the writer's purpose and the situation addressed in each case in order to permit the function of the idea in the intention of the one using it. As a result a wide range of meanings has become evident. Reflection upon these meanings in the materials surveyed enables us to draw several conclusions helpful toward an understanding of pre-existence as we approach the New Testament affirmations of the pre-existence of Christ.

First, the importance of the category of pre-existence for a particular philosophical or religious perspective is directly re-

---

[72] Jonas, *The Gnostic Religion,* p. 160.

lated to the intensity of the felt problem of man's relationship to the world in which he lives, whether that "world" be described as the human body, history, the universe, the earth, or society. If man is described as being more or less at home in his present existence, the category of pre-existence is modified, if indeed it appears at all. Where there is a strong sense of discontinuity between man and the world in which he lives—that is, between man and his present existence— there is a strong accent upon pre-existence. For example, in apocalyptic Judaism and in Gnosticism man is not at home; he is not in harmony with his present circumstance. He is a victim and needs deliverance from his tragic condition. Existence for man is so totally hopeless, whether the oppression be due to historical or spiritual powers, that relief must come from beyond existence. Any power able to save, or any condition of salvation, will come from outside existence. Hope lies in a condition of noncontingency, noninvolvement in this life. This means of redemption, or this state of redemption, lies in that realm before the tragedies of existence began, that is, in pre-existence.

As would be expected, the category of pre-existence has a modified function where life is understood, not as completely dark, but in terms of tension between good and evil. In other words, existence is not totally and essentially evil, and yet there is distance between the way things are and the way they were designed to be. On the one hand, a pre-existent being here serves to explain the good in existence by being an intermediary between the Ultimate Good and man's life. On the other hand, this being also serves to explain the distance between the Good and man, since an intermediate being, neither God nor man, would not only join the two but call attention to the vast gulf between them. Such is the function of pre-existence in the characterization of the Logos in Philo. In a sense this is also the function of Sophia in the Wisdom literature, for Sophia serves to explain "Godwardness" in all creation and in all nations, even though it is only in Israel that Wisdom has come to dwell.

Pre-existence has an even less significant function in those religious or philosophical perspectives which understand man's relation to the world to be one of continuity and harmony. Pre-existence is a stance outside existence prompted by a negative view of existence. If one's view of existence were positive, what need would there be for this category? Very little. Such, for example, is the case with Stoicism. For the Stoics, man is at home, in tune with the universe, by means of the all-pervading Logos. There is no realm of the "wholly other," for such would testify to the partial, incomplete nature of this universe. The Logos for the Stoics was not, therefore, a pre-existent being but rather a "dia-existent" principle. In a similar fashion, the Jewish rabbis had little need for the idea of pre-existence because they had a positive view of the universe. The universe is the creation of a benevolent God, and man, even though he transcends all else created, is a part of that creation. Man's body is neither a prison in which he is trapped nor an evidence of his fallenness, but man's body, like his soul, is the creation of God. Pre-existence stands in this theology more correctly as pre-destination, a dramatic way of affirming that everything has existed in the mind and will of

78

God from eternity. There is no final discontinuity, no ultimate conflict of eternal realities—all exists from the beginning in the will of the one God.

Second, the specific definition of pre-existence is determined in each case by the particular location of man's problem. This is to say, once the particular nature of the problem of human existence is located, pre-existence is defined in terms of that problem. If the human problem is in the realm of creation, the material world in which man is alien and pilgrim, then pre-existence would mean precreation. The system of Basilides is a good example of this pattern. For Basilides, man's problem is his existence, the fact that he is. The solution, imaged in the pre-existent state, is simply nonbeing. Pre-existence is therefore nonexistence, since before existence there was nonexistence. If, however, man's problem lies in the contradictions, abuses, injustices, and inequities of history, the answer to that problem is in the prehistorical or, in better terms, in the nonhistorical. The Son of Man in apocalyptic Judaism is nonhistorical; he is firmly and certainly set in prehistory. From another perspective man's basic problem may be his body, hindering and shackling the free spirit which has its home elsewhere. We would anticipate, therefore, that in such a view pre-existence would be specifically defined as preincarnation, pre-embodiment. To see man as he really is, one must see him in his essence before he falls, or is lured into, or foolishly accepts, this existence. This is the accent in Poimandres which unfolds the tragic tale of how heavenly Man became earthly man, and which preaches how man may again become Man.

The third and final conclusion to be drawn from this survey of uses of the idea of pre-existence in background materials is that the category of pre-existence demands a certain kind of language to convey it. To speak of pre-existence in the proper sense calls for the literary forms and images that belong to individuation. The Torah of the rabbis has an "ideal" existence in God's mind; it is predestined. The Logos of the Stoics pervades the totality of reality as universal or common reason; it is dia-existent. But ideas and principles do not pre-exist; they lack independence, individuality, the clear imagery that gives focus and identity. Apocalyptic Judaism and Gnosticism, on the other hand, convey the images of beings individual and distinct and in a realm entirely separate from observable and discoverable reality. Here we are dealing with myth. Mythology is the necessary language for expressing pre-existence.

We are prepared by these considerations to move now to the New Testament materials.

(2)

New Testament Affirmations
of the Pre-existence
# of Christ

The preceding survey of the meanings of pre-existence as presented in documents from the cultural and religious milieu of the New Testament produced essentially three conclusions. Summarily stated, they are as follows. First, the idea of pre-existence in all the documents testifies to the human spirit's tenacious capacity for transcendence. When caught in experiences of prolonged and radical discontinuity with the world in which they lived, men have sought meaning in "pretime," in pre-existence, before life fell into this tragic state. Rather than being reduced to victims of their present lot, they transcended hopeless history with myths of the primordial, refusing to believe man is no more than the sum of heredity and environment. Myths of pre-existence were affirmations of man's essence. This search for meaning was at the same time, therefore, a search for redemption, since it was anticipated that having run full cycle, the human spirit returned to become what it was.[1]

Second, wherever the sense of alienation from the world was sharpest, there also the dimension of pre-existence was most prominent. Many Hellenistic communities apparently experienced this alienation, for reasons already noted, while the people of Israel, firmly anchored to the doctrine of the creation of the world by a benevolent God, were not easily dislodged from positive views of this life and history. In Judaism, therefore, pre-existence is a minor consideration, even though Israel did not come through her darkest hours without theological modifications, as Jewish mystics and apocalypticists bear witness. Of course, when a culture had passed its crisis and had come upon calmer days, the world became "home" again. In such cases the idea of pre-existence, forged in the *angst* of a nightmare, lingered as a curious notion in the literature, prayers, and praise of the community. No one was interested to debate if pre-existence were "true"; it simply was no longer meaningful. Those who dwell comfortably in the high noon of tranquillity too easily mark as "odd" or "grotesque" the philosophical or theological or political structures of those who built during a dark night of terror.

Third, the category of pre-existence took a variety of forms, shaped in each particular document by the writer's definition of the human problem. One writer, regarding man's problem to be his body, would accent pre-existence as

---

[1] For an authoritative treatment of this perspective, cf. Mircea Eliade, *Cosmos and History,* trans. W. R. Trask (New York: Harper, 1959).

preincarnation while another, convinced that man's problem lay in the universe in which he lived, would define pre-existence as precreation. Since each writer's intention was so determinative, no single definition or understanding of pre-existence could be brought to the materials.

Having arrived at these conclusions, we must ask the question of whether or not they will serve to interpret the affirmations of pre-existence in the New Testament. Certainly the understandings of an idea in a general milieu would have bearing upon the understanding of that idea in documents produced in that milieu. But how direct a bearing? Can the reader of the New Testament anticipate these same definitions of pre-existence, or should he expect modifications?

Two facts about the content of New Testament materials make it clear that definite modifications in the idea of pre-existence will be present. In the first place, the New Testament attributes pre-existence not to all human spirits nor to an elect few, but to Christ alone.[2] It belongs to the limited area of Christology,[3] not to the general area of anthropology,[4] although these two considerations are not mutually exclusive, as will be noted later. The second fact about the New Testa-

---

[2] John 9:2 does not necessarily require the category of pre-existence for its interpretation.

[3] Of course, pre-existence in a sense is attributed to the kingdom and the saints (Matt. 25:34) after the manner of the Jewish rabbis (cf. chapter II). According to *Shepherd of Hermas* (Vis. II, 32-33) the church was the first of all creation.

[4] Anthropology provided the category of pre-existence for Christology, and then the church eliminated pre-existence as a valid category for anthropology. This separation of Christology and anthropology led to a great deal of misunderstanding.

ment message is that its central concern is with history.[5] It declares that God has acted in the concrete and discoverable history of a people and of a person. This fact alone virtually eliminates pre-existence as a meaningful category for understanding man's nature and purpose. The silence of the New Testament about the pre-existence of human spirits supports the logic of this conclusion. But would the attribution of pre-existence to the person of Christ be in any sense a contradiction of this central affirmation of the Christian faith? What did the writers intend to say about Christ when they spoke of him as pre-existent?

Any honest answers to these questions wait upon an examination of the texts. The method of the preceding chapter will be employed here; namely, an investigation of each writer's purpose, being open to the possibility that in the service of that purpose a writer may modify old meanings or create new ones. No one writer in the New Testament will define for all the writers the pre-existence of Christ. In fact, some variation may occur within the work of a given author.

Pre-existence in the Epistles of Paul. Paul was quite familiar with the idea of pre-existence and most likely made use of already available forms of the idea. It is unnecessary and unrealistic to suppose that he created this category, since pre-

---

[5] Soteriology structured on the line of history logically moves to an eschaton and final judgment, a predominant theme in the NT. But the cycle with the end returning to the beginning can also be seen in the NT, especially in Col. and Eph.

existence was a frame of reference already familiar to Paul's audiences. In fact, it is quite probable that Paul often quoted a poem, a hymn, or liturgical formula[6] already used in the Christian community to express the pre-existence of Christ.[7] It is also evident from his various uses of the idea of pre-existence that either Paul was familiar with several forms of the idea or he felt quite free to make radical modifications in it in order to establish his point.

And to what uses did Paul put his expressions of Christ's pre-existence? A preliminary reading of his most explicit statements of the pre-existence of Christ indicate that three major themes are developed by this dimension of Christology: (1) a pre-existent Christ is related not solely to redemption but to creation as well, so that these two realms are coextensive; (2) a pre-existent Christ who becomes existent reveals the necessary relationship between essence (who we are) and existence (how our lives are to be lived);[8] (3) a pre-existent Christ is not limited to the Christian era but figured in Israel's history as well, so that the life of Israel and the life

---

[6] As the subsequent discussion will clarify, many Pauline passages are so regarded; for example, Phil. 2:6-11; Col. 1:15-20; I Cor. 8:6.

[7] The Hellenistic church apart from Paul is difficult to characterize, but that the Hellenistic synagogue was a ripe soil for Paul's gospel is evident. Since Paul preached within one generation of the time of Jesus, the high Christologies of Paul's letters indicate the basic categories for such Christologies were already developed. There was not time for them to evolve from the church's experience of Jesus. Philo and Wis. of Sol. indicate the availability of these categories (Logos, Sophia, and Primal Man), not to mention sources in Hellenistic religions. See Bultmann, *Theology of the New Testament,* trans. Kendrick Grobel (New York: Scribner, 1951), Vol. I, ch. 3.

[8] I am aware that this traditional terminology is called into question by many contemporary writers. The problem will be discussed in chapter III.

of the church are strikingly parallel. Stated more briefly, the pre-existence of Christ is presented in relation to creation, to incarnation, and to history. To facilitate handling the materials, these three patterns will serve as the basic outline for the discussion.

Two of Paul's letters clearly exhibit his understanding of Christ as the mediator not only of the new creation,[9] but of the first as well. He says in I Cor. 8:5-6:

> For although there may be so-called gods in heaven and on earth —as indeed there are many "gods" and many "lords"—yet for us there is one God, the Father, from whom are all things and for whom we exist, and one Lord, Jesus Christ, through whom are all things and through whom we exist.

The other passage with this theme is Col. 1:15-20:

> He is the image of the invisible God, the first-born of all creation; for in him all things were created, in heaven and on earth, visible and invisible, whether thrones or dominions or principalities or authorities—all things were created through him and for him. He is before all things, and in him all things hold together. He is the head of the body, the church; he is the beginning, the first-born from the dead, that in everything he might be pre-eminent. For in him all the fullness of God was pleased to dwell, and through him to reconcile to himself all things, whether on earth or in heaven, making peace by the blood of his cross.

While these two passages are addressed to different con-

---

[9] II Cor. 5:17.

gregations with different problems and are not, therefore, to be forced into saying the same thing, still there are several reasons for looking at them together.[10] First, they have a common theme: Christ as mediator of creation and redemption. Second, they speak to a common theological problem: the belief on the part of the readers in the existence of many divine beings, referred to in I Corinthians as gods and lords and in Colossians as thrones, dominions, principalities, and authorities.[11] Third, they address a common religious problem: the worship of these powers, manifest in Corinth in attendance at shrines to idols[12] and in Colossae in the practice of angel worship.[13] Fourth, they have a common literary form. While the passage in Colossians is much longer, consisting of a hymn of two stanzas,[14] still both passages are in part structured

---

[10] In reaction against a "level" Bible, one must not so separate the epistles to the point of missing their common issues.

[11] For studies of these powers, cf. Hendrikus Berkhof, *Christ and the Powers,* trans. J. H. Yoder (Scottsdale, Pa.: Herald Press, 1962); G. B. Caird, *Principalities and Powers* (New York: Oxford University Press, 1956); Heinrich Schlier, *Principalities and Powers in the New Testament* (New York: Herder & Herder, 1961).

[12] I Cor. 8; 10. That the opponents of Paul in Corinth and Colossae were of one type, Gnostic Jews or Gnostic Jewish Christians, is a thesis well argued by W. Schmithals. Cf. his *Paul and James,* trans. D. M. Barton (Studies in Biblical Theology, No. 46; Naperville: Alec R. Allenson, 1965; German ed., 1963).

[13] Col. 2:18. Cf. F. W. Beare, *Interpreter's Bible,* XI, 140; Ernst Lohmeyer, *Die Briefe an die Kolosser und an Philemon* (Göttingen: Vandenhoeck & Ruprecht, 1956), pp. 6-7.

[14] The pioneer work on the hymnic character of this passage was done by E. Norden (*Agnostos Theos* [Leipzig: B. G. Teubner, 1913], pp. 250 ff.). For a list of formal analyses of the passage, cf. my article "All Things in Him," *New Testament Studies,* XII (1965), 78-80, n. 7.

upon a traditional Stoic formula which used a threefold construction of prepositional phrases.[15] This formula in various modifications is found also in Rom. 11:33*b*-35, Eph. 4:6, and Heb. 2:10.

Without a doubt the Christians in Corinth were not surprised by, nor did they have difficulty in accepting, the latter part of Paul's twofold statement concerning Christ: "through him we exist." Christ is the mediator of the new creation, the redeemer from death and bondage, the creator of the community of the "new beings." This truth was certified in their own experience; they knew what life had been for them previous to faith, and they knew what life meant now. In spite of all their moral irregularities (I Cor. 5;6), the congregational strife (I Cor. 1-3), and the abuses of their corporate life (I Cor. 8; 10-14), still the grace of God had been given to them in Christ Jesus, they had been enriched in him, and they were "not lacking in any spiritual gift" (I Cor. 1: 4-7). For all their disputes over the credentials of the minister who had first brought the gospel (I Cor. 9), there is no evidence in the letter that the Corinthians rejected Christ or doubted that "through him we exist."

But the first half of the Christological affirmation is quite different and raises a number of questions. The phrase "through whom are all things" refers to Christ's role as mediator of creation, an expression parallel to the earlier reference to God "from whom are all things," just as the work of Christ as mediator of redemption is parallel to the refer-

---

[15] Norden, *Agnostos Theos*, pp. 250 ff.

ence to God as the one "for whom we exist." That is, all things are *from* (creation) and *to* (redemption) God, but both creation and redemption are *through* Christ. The question is, why this affirmation that Christ was the agent of creation? Could this be simply a logical and normal extension, in doxological language, of the lordship of Christ over all things at all times? The Christian community, having experienced him as Redeemer, may be enlarging upon the implications of that experience. If Christ is Redeemer, then there can be no place nor force beyond his redemptive power, and therefore the realm of redemption must be coextensive with the realm of creation. Conclusion: the agent of redemption was agent also of creation. Such a direction in theological thought is not without precedent. The community of Israel had apparently thus reflected upon their experience of redemption in the Exodus and were able, because of it, to move theologically from redemption to creation and to affirm the Redeemer as Creator.[16]

While it may quite well be true that this was the pattern of a developing Christology, still this does not answer the basic question of the appropriateness at this particular point of an affirmation of Christ's pre-existence. The answer lies more deeply in the understanding of man's life in the universe which was held by some of the Corinthian Christians.

Paul was confronted in Corinth with a group who claimed

---

[16] This union of the redemption (Exodus) and creation themes is beautifully employed in Second Isaiah.

to be "of Christ" (I Cor. 1:12),[17] who were pneumatics or spiritualists[18] who felt they possessed the divine wisdom (1: 18-25)[19] and were perfect or mature (2:14–3:4). They had cut themselves loose from history. Being free and above material or earthly things, they dehistoricized Jesus and the resurrection to the point that Paul had to remind them of the fundamentals of the gospel: Christ died, was buried, and raised from the dead (15:1-11). They held to the primacy of the heavenly, as over against the earthly, man (15:45-49), a perspective common among many ancient cults and philosophies which regarded man as essentially a spirit, a heavenly spark, caught in the clay prison of the body. After all, thought the Corinthians, if the body is a temporary prison, it is quite foreign to man's true nature and the spirit's condition and may therefore be indulged without "spiritual" harm (5:1-2; 6:12-20). Such was the general orientation of these who were puffed up with knowledge (8:1-7).

These spiritualists with their knowledge of "reality" which enabled them to transcend the material world were apparently dualists; that is, they likely accounted for the two realms of

---

[17] James Moffatt, *The First Epistle of Paul to the Corinthians* (Moffatt New Testament Commentary; New York: Harper, 1938), pp. 10 ff. Also A. Robertson and A. Plummer, *ICC on First Epistle of Paul to the Corinthians* (Edinburgh: T. & T. Clark, 1914), pp. 12-13.

[18] W. Schmithals (*Die Gnosis in Korinth* [Göttingen: Vanderhoeck & Ruprecht, 1956], pp. 82-134) identifies them as Gnostics; so also U. Wilckens (*Weisheit and Torheit* [Tübingen: J. C. B. Mohr, 1959]). A contrary view is taken by J. Dupont (*Gnosis, la connaissance religieuse dans les épîtres de Saint Paul* [Louvain: E. Nauwelaerts, 1949]) and William Baird (*The Corinthian Church, a Biblical Approach to Urban Culture* [Nashville: Abingdon, 1964]).

[19] Hans Conzelmann, "Paulus und die Weisheit," *NTS*, XII (1966), 231 ff.

spirit and matter on the basis of two conflicting ultimate realities. There is no indication of how they accounted for the present nature of things with the combinations of spirit and matter that create man's agony and his need for redemption. Their attitude and behavior, however, reflected the conviction that the real essence of life is spirit while this existence is confinement. Knowing this truth, they felt they had already been raised and hence denied any future resurrection,[20] especially a bodily resurrection.[21]

Paul could not let this error stand unopposed, and the brief formula in I Cor. 8:6 is the summary of his entire answer. Christ does not redeem from the created order, from the body, from the material world. We have no problem with this existence as though it were from a demonic source, nor is this life a condition of fallenness from our true spiritual essence. All things, whether visible or invisible, of heaven or earth, of the spirit world or the material world, have the same source. The one through whom we have redemption is the same one through whom all things were created. Creation has its fulfillment in redemption; redemption is the experience providing the proper understanding of creation. The pre-existent Christ is involved in existence by his act of creation and by his act of redemption.

Although both creation and redemption are themes of this brief confession, clearly the accent is upon creation; the af-

---

[20] I Cor. 15:12-19. Paul at times interprets resurrection as a past experience for Christians (Rom. 6:1-11), but he keeps an eschatological reservation.
[21] I Cor. 15:35-50.

firmation has its primary focus upon the origin of all things. There is one Lord because of creation, and the one Lord is Jesus Christ because all things had their beginning through him. The Stoic formula upon which this Christian confession is framed ("from . . . , through . . . , unto . . .") assumes the cyclical view of reality: the end will be a return to the beginning. Paul does not here develop the rather subdued redemption theme. This he does elsewhere, as will be seen in the Colossian passage to be examined below. He merely says, "through whom we exist." The dimensions of the realm of redemption are not an immediate concern. Apparently the formula is chosen because it expresses what he wishes at this point to affirm about Christ: the mediator of our redemption is the mediator of all creation. The statement embraces all things; no person or power exists outside it. There is one Lord, Jesus Christ, because of creation.

Careful readers of Paul detect here some real tension with the Christology in I Cor. 15.[22] In that chapter the focus is not upon the creation, the beginning of all things. Rather the orientation is toward the eschaton, the parousia of Christ. Without explaining how there has come to be hostility and enmity (15:24-26) in a world where all things owe their existence to Christ, Paul declares there will be one Lord at the parousia. Christ *will be* Lord over all things (15:27-28). If

---

[22] Of course there is the problem of the integrity of I Corinthians, but even that will not resolve this tension because even if chs. 8 and 15 are different letters, Paul wrote both. On the problem of integrity, cf. Paul Feine and Johannes Behm, *Introduction to the New Testament*, ed. W. G. Kümmel, trans. A. J. Mattill, Jr. (Nashville: Abingdon, 1966), pp. 202-205.

the confession in 8:6 was framed on the cycle familiar to the Hellenistic world, here in chapter 15 the Christology is framed on the line of history familiar to Judaism. Both the cycle and the line appear in Paul. When one backs off to look at Paul's thought as a whole, the two perspectives relieve each other: the cycle provides a larger context for viewing history; the line shatters the acosmic inevitability of the cycle. But the point here is that Paul frames his Christology at any given point so as to meet the issue at hand. To this extent his Christology is functional; he does not move with a systematic on all fronts at once.[23] Had such been his aim, he probably would have sought to negotiate carefully the tension between I Cor. 8 and 15.

The fact is, in I Cor. 8:6 Paul apparently has no eye on the problem later to be addressed. His immediate concern is the affirmation which best addresses those Corinthians whose attitude toward this world reflects a flaw in understanding the creation in relation to Christ. If pre-existence (the heavenly is antecedent to the earthly) had been for the Corinthians a basis for a negative stance toward the created order, Paul radically modified that idea of pre-existence. While for the Corinthian pneumatics the true and the essential realm of reality, pre- and supraexistent, was the realm of spirit apart from the present existent world, Paul unites the two realms. This he does, not by elevating matter to the realm

---

[23] Paul may not have been the only one redacting and modifying the tradition. Perhaps some of the Corinthians were doing the same.

of the eternal,[24] but by affirming that all things, spirit and matter, belong to the order of the created, having a common source through a common mediator. Regardless of how unbelievers may look upon the universe, whether they regard it as dualistic or pluralistic (many gods and many lords), "yet for us there is one God, the Father, from whom are all things and for whom we exist, and one Lord, Jesus Christ, through whom are all things and through whom we exist."

As stated above there are a number of striking similarities between the poetic formula of I Cor. 8:6 and the Christological hymn in Col. 1:15-20. The two stanzas of this hymn expand upon the two aspects of the work of Christ as found in I Corinthians: he is mediator of creation and of redemption. There is, however, a strikingly different accent in this passage, as will be noted later.

It is difficult to reconstruct the nature of the heresy Paul addressed at Colossae.[25] Apparently a heterodox (Gnostic?) Jewish group that had embraced Christianity brought with them feasts, fasts, new moon celebrations, sabbaths (Col. 2: 16-18) and ordinances of the Law (2:14). However, these practices were conducted with an orientation toward the spirit powers which lay back of this earthly existence with its material limitations (2:8, 20). These powers, variously called thrones, principalities, dominions, and authorities (1:

---

[24] As did the pantheistic Stoics.

[25] For two quite different characterizations, cf. J. B. Lightfoot, *St. Paul's Epistles to the Colossians and to Philemon* (London: Macmillan, 1879) and Günther Bornkamm, "Die Häresie des Kolosserbriefes," *Das Ende des Gesetzes* (München: Chr. Kaiser Verlag, 1952), pp. 139 ff.

16), and collectively referred to as angels (2:18), were wor-
shiped, apparently because they lay in the realm of the invisible and had power touching the essence of one's true being.
With apparent disdain for this bodily existence, these Colossians were caught up in visions (2:18),[26] enjoyed the mysteries of wisdom and knowledge (2:3), and sought to abolish
the senses of the body by stern asceticism, starving all bodily
appetites by the self-imposed regulation, "Do not handle, Do
not taste, Do not touch" (2:21). This asceticism was another
way of responding to the same view of the material dimensions of life which had produced libertinism in Corinth. Asceticism and libertinism are symptoms of the same erroneous
view of the material order. Thus, as he had responded to the
Corinthians, Paul hurled at these "puffed up" (2:18) per-
verters of the gospel his defense of the faith.

It is important to note that the central and governing consideration of these Colossians was the spirit world with its
plurality of "elemental spirits of the universe." It apparently
was not intended that these powers replace Christ as the object
of worship but rather that they supplement his work in order
to make redemption complete.[27] These powers brought fulfillment (2:10) to the devotee. The inadequacy of Christ's
redemptive work was demonstrated, they felt, in the fact
that he suffered and died. Paul is quite aware that assigning
to Christ a role of relative significance is a more serious threat

---

[26] This is an enigmatic phrase. Some conjectures are: "standing on what is
not seen"; "standing on the air"; "hovering in between on emptiness."

[27] On this point see W. L. Knox, *St. Paul and the Church of the Gentiles*,
pp. 150-52.

to the faith of the Christian community than would be a flat denial. He is concerned also to demonstrate that the passion of Christ was not tragedy and defeat but the very event of triumph over every contrary force (2:13-15).

The hymn in Col. 1:15-20 affirms, therefore, the work of Christ primarily in relation to these powers of the spirit world. This work of Christ involves both creation and redemption, but unlike I Cor. 8:6, the scope of Christ's work is enlarged to embrace these powers. This is an interesting extension of thought beyond the affirmation in I Corinthians. There, when Paul spoke of Christ's redemptive work, he included only the historical Christian community; that is, "through whom *we* exist," as contrasted to the scope of Christ's creative work, "through whom are *all things*." In that letter Paul later stated that the final relationship of "all things" to Christ will be subjection and subordination (15:27-28). In so doing, Christ will destroy[28] all hostile power in the universe. However, in Colossians "all things," including every created order in heaven and on earth, invisible as well as visible, will be redeemed, reconciled in Christ (1:20; 2:19).[29] In fact, Christ is the head of these powers and they are to be part of his church, pictured as a cosmic body (1:18).[30]

---

[28] *Katargeo.* However, "destruction" need not mean annihilation of the powers but destruction of the independent power of the powers, thus restoring them to their proper place.

[29] This idea of reconciliation is not a contradiction of I Cor. 15:24 as explained in n. 28. above. Cf. Caird, *Principalities and Powers*, p. 83.

[30] In spite of the fact that Col. 1:18*a* belongs with the first stanza of the hymn and thus embraces the whole creation, some scholars argue for the church

On what basis can Paul project such a grand view of cosmic reconciliation? [31] He does so on the basis of Christ's work as mediator of creation. What was implicit in Paul's expression "through whom are all things" in I Corinthians is here made explicit. These powers which the Colossians understood as granting fulfillment of life were themselves created in, through, and for Christ. In fact, it is in him that the totality of creation coheres (1:17). As the mediator of creation is pre-existent, all else is existent, created being, and finds its unity in him who stands before and beyond all the contingencies and changes characteristic of the created order.[32]

However, if Paul had said only this, he could be cited as providing support for those who turn from matter and body and seek their salvation in the eternal realm outside existence, for such a Christ could be counted as the spirit power par excellence, the one above and beyond all others. Hence it is important to turn again to the second stanza of the hymn and notice that Christ's act of redeeming and reconciling all things is "by the blood of his cross" (1:20). The cross firmly fixes the central event of the purposes of God for the whole

---

in Paul as always a historical community. Cf. Eduard Schweizer, *The Church as the Body of Christ* (Richmond: John Knox, 1964). For a summary of the debate, cf. S. Hanson, *The Unity of the Church in the New Testament* (Uppsala: Almquist and Wiksells, 1946).

[31] An excellent treatment of the scope of Christ's work is found in A. D. Galloway, *The Cosmic Christ* (New York: Harper, 1951). Also Emmanuel McIver, "The Cosmic Dimensions of Salvation in the Thought of St. Paul," *Worship*, XL (1966), 156-64.

[32] A. Feirillet, "La création de l'univers dans le Christ d'après l'épître aux Colossiens (1:16*a*)" *NTS*, XII (1965), 1 ff.

creation in the *terra firma* of history. Redemption has been accomplished within history, in the empirical world of human affairs, and does not lie in the visions and speculations focused upon the complexities of the heavenly order.

The Redeemer of all things is Creator of all things; the Creator of all things is Redeemer of all things. This is more than theological and literary symmetry: it is a rebuke and a corrective for all who consciously or unconsciously subscribe to the Colossian heresy. If all things are in him, through him, and for him, then the material world did not have some dark and demonic origin. That life which seeks salvation through the pleasurable rigors of not handling, not tasting, not touching is not only caught in futile will-worship, but is guilty of an implicit insult to the Creator of all things.[33]

In addition to his use of affirmations of Christ's pre-existence to demonstrate that creation and redemption are twin doctrines that have their center in Christ, Paul also speaks of Christ's pre-existence to join essence and existence, to explain to his converts the real meaning of life, its essence, discovered and expressed in the context of their day-by-day existence. He explains what it means to be in Christ here and now, in the business of being a Christian where men are under any and all circumstances. He does so by reminding his readers of the incarnation, the coming into existence of the pre-existent, in whom one discovers and is apprehended by the true nature, the essence, of the authentic life. In Christ

---

[33] Yet one suspects this negative piety charmed the immature into terming such behavior "saintliness."

there is manifest in history, in time, now, the nature of life eternal. This is what is meant by saying that the pre-existent and existent Christ expresses essence within existence.[34]

There are two such affirmations in Paul's letters. In II Cor. 8:9 he wrote: "For you know the grace of our Lord Jesus Christ, that though he was rich, yet for your sake he became poor, so that by his poverty you might become rich." In a similar vein, with equal beauty of thought and expression, he wrote to the Philippians:

Have this mind among yourselves, which you have in Christ Jesus, who, though he was in the form of God, did not count equality with God a thing to be grasped, but emptied himself, taking the form of a servant, being born in the likeness of men. And being found in human form he humbled himself and became obedient unto death, even death on a cross. Therefore God has highly exalted him and bestowed on him the name which is above every name, that at the name of Jesus every knee should bow, in heaven and on earth and under the earth, and every tongue confess that Jesus Christ is Lord, to the glory of God the Father. (2:5-11)

As I Cor. 8:6 and Col. 1:15-20 had much in common, so do these two passages. First, they have a common theme, the entering into existence of the pre-existent Christ. Just as in the two previously considered passages pre-existence meant

---

[34] The reader will recognize here the now familiar terminology of Paul Tillich, who often spoke of Christ as "essence under the conditions of existence."

precreation, so here pre-existence stands for preincarnation. Second, these two passages are framed upon a common imagery or pattern, the descent and ascent of the Redeemer. In the briefer expression in II Corinthians, the formula presents the descent of the Redeemer in order to effect the ascent of the saints. In Philippians the Redeemer descends, then ascends, or rather is exalted, and as a consequence all created beings praise him as Lord. Third, both passages present the drama of the Christ event in order to speak to very practical problems in the congregations: in the one case, to encourage and to urge an offering for the poor; in the other, to settle tensions and discord in the church at Philippi. In other words, both passages are employed by Paul as a pastoral theologian, not as an academic theologian. And finally, both these affirmations are noticeably poetic and are the compositions of a writer or writers[35] quite conscious of literary style. Especially is the hymnic form of Phil. 2:6-11 evident, with its three movements: the pre-existent Christ with the Father; the descent and humiliation; the ascent and exaltation of the Christ.[36]

At the point of immediate concern in II Corinthians, Paul

---

[35] There is some question as to whether Paul is the composer of these passages; he may be quoting from materials already familiar to the churches. Cf. Beare (*Interpreter's Bible*, XI, 142-45) for the debate.

[36] For a bibliography of formal analyses of this hymn, cf. F. W. Beare, *The Epistle to the Philippians* (Harper New Testament Commentaries; New York: Harper, 1959), pp. 41-42. Of course not all scholars agree there are three movements in the hymn; some find only two. For a survey of these analyses, cf. R. P. Martin, *An Early Christian Confession* (London: Tyndale, 1960), pp. 7 ff. For the criteria for detecting traditional formulas, cf. R. H. Fuller, *Foundations of New Testament Christology*, pp. 20-21.

is engaged in a matter familiar to every pastor, the raising of funds. Among the Gentile churches Paul is collecting an offering for the saints in Judea, the Jewish Christians who have been victimized by a famine in southern Palestine.[37] The offering is extremely important not only for the relief it will bring to those distressed, nor only for the spiritual benefits it will bring to those who share; but for Paul it will be an expression of good faith and brotherliness reaching across the widening gulf between Jewish and Gentile Christianity. When Paul and fellow missionaries to the Gentiles met in Jerusalem with Peter and fellow missionaries to the Jews, their parting was with a handclasp and with a word: "Remember the poor" (Gal. 2:1-10). This Paul has done, and is doing, with persistent efforts, for the matter involved is not economic, although he surely knows how real are the pangs of hunger. The matter involved is no less than the nature of the church, her unity, her fellowship, her entire understanding of what it means for a community to be called out from a variety of backgrounds to be "in Christ." [38] If Jews and Gentiles share in spiritual blessings, then they share as well in material blessings (Rom. 15:27). There can be no

---

[37] The offering is elsewhere referred to by Paul in Rom. 15:25-27; I Cor. 16:1-4. Again the question of the integrity of II Corinthians raises the issue of whether chs. 8 and 9 belong to one letter. The present study is not materially affected by it, but for a discussion of the problem, cf. W. H. Bates, "The Integrity of II Corinthians," *NTS*, XII (1965), 56 ff.

[38] Schmithals, *Paul and James*, pp. 79-84. Also Keith F. Nickle, *The Collection* (Studies in Biblical Theology, No. 48; London: SCM Press, 1966), pp. 100-143.

division of life into two parts—brothers in spirit but quite unrelated in such material and mundane matters as food and clothing. All of life, spiritual and material, is included in that life within the community of those in Christ.

It comes, therefore, as no real surprise, in view of the magnitude of the issue at hand, that Paul inserts into the heart of his discussion of money a brief but profound summary of the entire gospel, the event of Jesus Christ. The formula used (whether quoted or Paul's own is not vital here) is in terms appropriate to the occasion: Christ was rich but for your sakes became poor in order that you might become rich.

Two words of caution are needed here. First, one must not allow this passage to be taken as meaning that the moving and compelling force of the gospel story is to be found in the financial poverty of Christ. In other words, the Word which moves men to God is not a dramatic recitation of the privations in the life of Jesus. It is true that men, especially those in affluence and comfort, are touched by awe, pity, and guilt when reminded of the conditions under which Jesus lived: the manger, the poor offering of turtle doves at his dedication, no place to lay his head, and the paucity of personal possessions to be shared by his crucifiers. And, of course, it is true that the Gospel of Luke tells his story with obvious sympathy for the poor, the have-nots, with whom Jesus identified. Mary sang, says Luke, praise to God in anticipation of the birth, for "he has filled the hungry with good things, and the rich he has sent empty away" (1:53). However, in spite of all the idealizing and spiritualizing of poverty as a blessed condition,[39] as though a man's life consisted of the things he did *not* possess, still the gospel cannot be equated with the poverty of Jesus any more than it can be equated with the pain of Jesus on the cross. This is a cheapening of the Christ event and a mishandling of Paul, who never uses data from the life of Jesus as the basis for paraenesis. The fact that Paul is, in this particular passage, involved in discussing financial matters should not necessarily cause one to interpret the Christ event economically. The fact is, Paul understood what many who quote this passage do not; namely, that Christology belongs to the substructure of Christian faith and is therefore more appropriate to the offering than is the immediate financial leverage there may be in a reference to Christ's poverty.

A second caution at this point is against the understanding of this passage as meaning that the gospel story is a simple business transaction: poor now, rich later; give now, collect later. It is a distortion of Christianity that reduces the gospel to a strategy for getting ultimately one's own way and attaining one's own goals.

What, then, does the passage mean? It is a brief, poetic résumé of the Christ drama structured upon the rich-poor contrast to convey that which is often spatially pictured as above-below, heaven-earth, or, in more philosophical terms,

---

[39] Classic examples are to be found in Augustine, *Sermons on New Testament Lessons;* Philip Schaff, *Nicene and Post-Nicene Fathers* VI, 449; Aquinas, "Of Christ's Manner of Life," *Summa Theologica,* English Dominican translation, II, 2238; Calvin, *Second Epistle of Paul the Apostle to the Corinthians,* comment on II Cor. 8:9.

the pre-existent become existent, the essential come under the conditions of existence.[40] The word "rich" describes that estate of the pre-existent Christ which elsewhere is described as the Son's "glory which I had with thee before the world was made" (John 17:5) and as "equality with God" (Phil. 2:6). Becoming "poor" does not refer to becoming penniless but rather to the whole event of the incarnation, the eternal under conditions of time, the noncontingent being made subject to all the contingencies of human experiences. Paul here is describing what he elsewhere described as emptying himself (Phil. 2:7) and being "born of woman, born under the law" (Gal. 4:4). In fact, "poor" and "empty" have very similar meanings and may on occasion be used interchangeably.[41]

As will be pointed out in the discussion of Phil. 2:6-11, for the Christ to become poor or to empty himself means for him to come under the "elemental spirits of the universe," the powers that determine the character of human existence.[42] The nature of the human condition is presented by Paul in Gal. 4:1-11. Paul's adversaries were involved in a heterodox (perhaps Gnostic) Judaism, in pursuit of which they observed fasts, sabbaths, and new moons. In addition, they were in bondage to the Law and its requirements, which for Paul

---

[40] Apparently *ploutos* (rich) describes the realm of the Father; *ptochos* (poor) and *kenos* (empty), the realm of the elemental powers.

[41] I Cor. 15:10. The variant reading "poor" instead of "empty" or "vain" occurs in D* (G) it.

[42] Paul used these categories Christologically; the Gnostics used them anthropologically. For example, Gospel of Thomas, Logia 2, 30, 107 (according to numbering of logia by R. M. Grant and D. N. Freedman in *Secret Sayings of Jesus* [New York: Doubleday, 1960]).

was bondage to the elemental powers of the universe, beings which by nature are not gods. Such legalism, such orientation toward observances, restrictions, and prohibitions, belonged to the childhood, the slave stage of life. God has acted, however, in that he "sent forth his Son, born of woman, born under the law, to redeem those who were under the law, so that we might receive adoption as sons. . . . So through God you are no longer a slave but a son, and if a son then an heir" (Gal 4:4-5, 7). Christ came under the conditions of our existence, under the powers that Paul described with the same word used in II Cor. 8:9 to speak of Christ's redemptive coming: they are "poor" (Gal. 4:9).[43]

Thus did the rich one become poor; the pre-existent Christ, free and sovereign over all the created powers of the universe, came under those powers, tasting the full measure of their thrust, even to the cross.[44] In so doing, he has made his disciples rich; that is, "no longer a slave but a son, and if a son then an heir." The Christian community even now enjoys that richness, purchased by his poverty, which is marked by an authentic freedom and sovereignty over the formerly enslaving created order. In fact, now, in the conditions of existence, the believers possess that life which is here presented as the pre-existent condition of Christ: he was rich. In the

---

[43] E. D. Burton's explanation of the elements of the universe as the fundamentals of religion, the ABC's, is inadequate as a treatment of the elemental powers in Paul (*A Critical and Exegetical Commentary on the Epistle to the Galatians* [Edinburgh: T. & T. Clark, 1921], pp. 510 ff.) For another view, see H. Schlier, *Der Brief an die Galater* (Meyer's *Kommentar*; Göttingen: Vandenhoeck & Ruprecht, 1951), pp. 131 ff.

[44] I Cor. 2:8.

midst of life now they experience that eternity which, in the categories of Pauline language, is pre-existent; that is, it is of the essence of reality. Paul had said to the Corinthians in an earlier letter: "For all things are yours, whether Paul or Apollos or Cephas or the world or life or death or the present or the future, all are yours; and you are Christ's; and Christ is God's" (I Cor. 3:21b-23). "Already you are filled! Already you have become rich!" (I Cor. 4:8.)

If Paul is quoting a Christological formula in II Cor. 8:9, there is as yet no way of recovering its earlier context. It is evident, however, that here it stands as a reminder to the Christians in Corinth of that event of God's grace by which they are now alive and rich. But being in Christ is not a life of mystic communion and ecstatic elevation above the mundane. The drama of redemption is not to the end that they escape existence, but that in the context of existence they encounter, or rather are encountered by, life itself. This drama took place where they lived, in history, in Jesus of Nazareth. Therefore express it where you live, says Paul, in the circumstances of each day's life—for example, in the sharing of one's purse with those in need. In order to create a community of persons able thus to share all of life, spiritual and material, he who was rich became poor. The doctrines of creation and incarnation agree in affirming one truth: there is no separation of a spiritual realm from a material realm. There are not two worlds; there is but one "in him."

The other passage in which Paul affirms Christ's pre-existence in such a way as to mean preincarnation is Phil. 2:6-11. It has been considered already, directly and indirectly, because of its close similarity to II Cor. 8:9, but it should be examined briefly in its own context and in the service of Paul's particular purpose in that letter.[45]

The church at Philippi, with whom Paul enjoyed a happy and mutually fruitful relationship, was plagued by some internal tension and discord. The strife had not only broken out in open disagreement between two members (4:2-3), but, as is usually the case, all or most of the congregation had been affected (2:1-5). Whether or not this was the work of some particular faction of agitators, heretical in behavior if not in theology (1:15, 28, 30; 3:2, 18-20), is not clear.[46] Paul's concern, however, was not solely with this tension and its attendant grumbling (2:14), but with a more subtly divisive force in the church—individualism. Individualism, upon which the Greek culture put a premium, was a real threat to community life, upon which both Judaism and Christianity were built. This individualism, operating behind the rather respectable screen of "each minding his own business," was paralyzing the church experience (2:4). With tender firmness Paul appeared for unity and concord, in the course of which he presented (quoted) a Christological hymn.[47]

After a brief introduction ("Think this among yourselves which also you think in Christ Jesus"[48]), Paul sang of him who was in the form of God, who came to earth, who de-

---

[45] Or letters. On the integrity of Philippians, cf. Beare, *Philippians*, pp. 1 ff. Also T. E. Pollard, "The Integrity of Philippians," *NTS*, XIII (1966), 57-65.

[46] W. Schmithals, "Die Irrlehrer des Philipperbriefes," *ZTK*, LIV (1957), 297-341.

[47] See n. 36 above.

[48] Translation mine.

scended into the grave, and who had been exalted and acclaimed as Lord of all beings in heaven, on earth, and in the netherworld. The Christ who was in heaven, on earth, and, through death, in the netherworld, extended his reign to all creation since in the language of that day these three realms constituted the totality of the universe. In three dramatic movements the whole event of God's grace in Christ had been portrayed. But why all this to address a problem of congregational discord? It seems that Paul brought in a theological cannon to shoot a very ordinary rabbit. What has pre-existence to do with the problem or its solution?

It is apparent that in the use of a Christological formula to speak to a practical problem in the church, the situation here is very similar to that noted in II Cor. 8:9. It is very easy, therefore, to let the practical nature of the problem mislead the student into viewing the Christological material in a way too utilitarian.[49] On the one hand, it is true that here is a clear reminder that the context and function of theology is within the church as it both addresses and expresses the community's life and faith. On the other, however, to think of theology in utilitarian ways, to dismiss as irrelevant those directions and dimensions of Christian theology which do not directly and immediately answer a question, meet a need, solve a problem, raise a budget, or create a sermon, is a prostitution of the province and scope of Christian thought. A premature or hasty demand for relevance paralyzes thought

---

[49] As I think John Harvey has done in "A New Look at the Christ Hymn in Phil. 2:6-11," *Expository Times*, LXXVI (1965), 337-39.

which could, in the larger perspective, prove to be the most relevant after all. Paul is here a pastor bringing to bear upon a local problem a Christological affirmation which most likely was formulated under other circumstances allowing for more theological reflection. It proves to be most relevant here, but the reader, anxious to find its relevance, may miss the meaning of the hymn by pressing it into immediate service.

It is, therefore, a violation of Paul's use of the hymn to fragment the Christ event into acts and attitudes to be reproduced in the life of the believer. For example, cutting the passage into hortatory pieces has led to such misunderstandings as, "Be like the humble Jesus." A careful reading of verses 6 through 11 makes it clear that Paul was not discussing the earthly career of Jesus at all. The life and ministry of the historical Jesus are not an ethical example in Paul.[50] The humiliation here spoken of was the entrance into existence and submission to the conditions of existence by the pre-existent Christ. An understanding of the hymn's theme of Christ's humiliation and exaltation in directly moral and ethical terms could put the interpreter in the position of advocating a highly questionable ethic; that is, the use of humility as a strategy for attaining exaltation.

Neither was Paul saying, "Think as Jesus thought." Such an interpretation reflects more of the subjectivism and internalization of this generation than of the meaning of the

---

[50] Schweizer, *Lordship and Discipleship*, p. 99. The best treatment of Phil. 2:6-11 raising the question of whether pre-existence is involved is that of C. H. Talbert in "The Problem of Pre-existence in Phil. 2:6-11," *JBL*, LXXXVI (1967), 141 ff. However, this historicization of the hymn is also unconvincing.

writer. Admittedly verse 5 is difficult to translate, but apparently Paul was saying that the mind or attitude or orientation of the church in its community experience, in the relationships of members with each other, should reflect the real meaning of what it is to be "in Christ Jesus." What followed, then, was a rehearsal of the entire Christ event which had made possible their new life and community, a rehearsal of that which, because of its familiarity, could so easily be forgotten.

What Paul did, therefore, was to remind his readers of the locus of the Christian life; they lived "in Christ Jesus," and their being "in him" had been made possible by the entire salvation drama. The passage is not directly ethical, but rather the ethical problem Paul addressed is set within the larger context of soteriology, the meaning of salvation.[51] He was saying, "Show where you live (in Christ Jesus) by how you live (with each other in Philippi)."

With this function of the passage in mind, the hymn itself can be seen as a unit. The motif is essentially the same as in II Cor. 8:9, but with greater elaboration. The Christ as Redeemer not only left his pre-existent state to come to earth, but descended also into the lower regions and then returned, exalted as Lord of all created beings. The humiliation of Christ was thus complete; his identification with the human situation was without reservation. He became subject to the powers of this age who put him to death on the cross.[52] As

---

[51] Beare, *Philippians*, p. 75. Also Karl Barth, *The Epistle to the Philippians*, trans. J. W. Leitch (Richmond: John Knox, 1962), pp. 50-68.

[52] So Beare (*Philippians*, p. 84) but not Barth (*Philippians*, pp. 64-65).

Paul dramatically expressed it in I Cor. 2:8: "None of the rulers of this age [meaning the demons, the powers and principalities] understood this; for if they had, they would not have crucified the Lord of glory." By his death, Christ's becoming "empty" or "poor" was made complete.[53]

The extension of Christ's lordship and redemption to the netherworld [54] is a New Testament theme the universalism of which has, in the Western church, been overshadowed by the more Judaic emphasis upon a final judgment with a separation of the good and evil. In the Western church tradition, wherever the idea of a lower region inhabited by the dead or by spirit powers has survived, it has usually been thought of as beyond the reach of the salvation event. This is not the case, according to this passage. This dimension of Christ's work, expressed in the Apostles' Creed by the now enigmatic "he descended into Hades," is presented not only here but elsewhere in the New Testament. In Eph. 4:8-9 Christ is described as descending into the lower parts of the earth, making captive the powers, and then ascending to his place of lordship over all things.[55] Likewise in I Peter 3:18-22 Christ, upon his death, descended into Hades, there ministered, and then rose to his

---

[53] In Paul the incarnation is a kenosis; in John and I Tim. 3:16 the incarnation is an epiphany.

[54] Justin, *Dialogue with Trypho* 88:5; 140:4; 141:1; *Second Apology* 5:2; also Ignatius' letters, Ephesians 13:2; 19:1, 2; Trallians 9:1; Smyrnaeans 6:1; and the Gospel of Peter V:39-42.

[55] Bultmann (*Theology of the New Testament*, II, 151-52) regards this as a reference to the earth, not hades as in I Peter 3:18-22. For the view that the ascension *preceded* the descent, cf. Calvin Porter, "The Descent of Christ," *One Faith*, ed. R. L. Simpson (Enid, Okla.: Phillips University Press, 1966), pp. 45-58.

111

place of lordship with all angels, authorities, and powers subject to him. The totality is included; the realm of his lordship is coextensive with the realm of creation. After all, if it is man's situation in the world to be threatened by the powers of evil that thwart the purposes of God and alienate man from God, even to separation in death, then redemption that is truly redemption must deliver from all hostile forces. A Lord who is truly Lord can tolerate no dark corners in the universe unreached by his power. Christ, having moved through the three spheres of the created order, completed his mission. "Therefore God has highly exalted him and bestowed on him the name which is above every name, that at the name of Jesus every knee should bow, in *heaven* and on *earth* and *under the earth*, and every tongue confess that Jesus Christ is Lord, to the glory of God the Father." (Phil. 2:9-11.)

Thus did Paul recite the drama of salvation, not as ethical precepts to be followed, but as a description of what it meant for the church to be "in Christ Jesus," to participate in this victory and to live in this freedom. Within the conditions and contingencies of existence, in history, the divine had invaded the human; eternity had moved into time. To share in that event is to live in an eternal now; in time, but not in bondage to time; in the body, but not "according to the flesh."

Within this doxological affirmation of Christ's redeeming work there lay embedded an inescapable imperative which apparently had not struck the Philippians: the necessity, in their community experience, of translating "in Christ Jesus" into "in Philippi."

112

So far it has been noted that Paul used the idea of pre-existence in the sense of precreation in order to establish that Christ is the agent of creation, thereby enabling the readers to see creation and redemption as one, having their center in Christ. This was particularly vital to a community with a background in a dualism which was oriented negatively toward the material world. It has also been seen that Paul used the pre-existence motif in a sense of preincarnation in order to point out that the Christ event within observable history was to reveal and to make accessible the nature of reality, the very essence of authentic life. This Christ accomplished by leaving the realms of eternity and noncontingent being to enter the realm of the contingent, where he subjugated and brought into their proper place as created beings all the forces which had enslaved man in a peripheral life of service to created and transient things, worshiping what by nature were not gods. In a historical event man has been confronted by the act of God's grace, and so he has become redeemed man here and now. However, since the event of grace was of the Eternal in that the pre-existent came from elsewhere into the world ("God sent forth his Son"), man as redeemed man is not *subject* to the here and now.[56]

There is yet a third way, quite distinct from the two already considered, in which Paul conceived of pre-existence. In this use of the idea Paul relates the pre-existent Christ to two widely separated events on the time line of history. It is interesting to note that while this third conception of pre-

---

[56] Note the Pauline antithesis expressing this freedom, II Cor. 6:9-10.

existence occurs in I Corinthians, it could not be discussed in connection with I Cor. 8:6 because the category here is structured quite differently and serves an entirely different function. Such differing views and uses of the same general frame of reference within the same letter [57] are further reminders that the function of an idea in the purpose of a writer is the primary criterion for defining that idea. The passage is I Cor. 10:1-4:

> I want you to know, brethren, that our fathers were all under the cloud, and all passed through the sea, and all were baptized into Moses in the cloud and in the sea, and all ate the same supernatural food and all drank the same supernatural drink. For they drank from the supernatural Rock which followed them, and the Rock was Christ.

There is no need to sketch again here the conditions Paul addressed in this letter and the particular perspectives upon life and the Christian faith held by the pneumatics in the church in Corinth. That picture was drawn earlier in connection with I Cor. 8:6. It need only be said that Paul was quite aware that the presumption on the part of these "mature ones" that they were secure in their transcendence over the problems that beset the immature carried within it spiritual doom. They needed to be warned sternly that they had not yet "arrived." Paul issued this warning "to take heed lest they fall" in the form of two analogies.

---

[57] See n. 22 above.

In the first analogy Paul compared the life of the Christian to that of the athlete. The athlete brings to the contest a background of rigorous discipline and self-control, knowing "that in a race all the runners compete, but only one receives the prize. So run that you may obtain it" (9:24). Paul knew that even in his own case this self-discipline was essential, "lest after preaching to others I myself should be disqualified" (9:27).

The second analogy was drawn from the history of Israel. Addressing an audience predominantly Gentile, or perhaps from Hellenistic Judaism, Paul interpreted the history of Israel typologically.[58] The wilderness experience of Israel is presented as a type of the Christian experience. Israel, like the Corinthians, had her initiation by baptism, followed by a continuing experience of the spiritual (supernatural) meal. However, her "baptism" and "communion" gave to Israel no immunity against temptations to idolatry, frivolity, and sexual immorality, as the wilderness tragedies grimly testified. So let the presumptuous Corinthians beware.

It is in this context that Paul spoke of the pre-existent Christ. According to the Old Testament, the children of Israel drank from a rock which became for them a fountain in the wilderness (Exod. 17:6; Num. 20:11). The story of the rock grew through generations of storytelling into a legend about the rock which followed Israel through the

---

[58] The Corinthian church possibly had a Hellenistic Jewish background, or the OT was interpreted typologically to instruct Gentile converts. L. Goppelt, "Paulus und die Heilsgeschichte," *NTS*, XIII (1966), 31-42.

desert as an ever present source of water.[59] This legend was apparently widely known and in the hands of various writers received modifications and elaborations. In the apocryphal book Wisdom of Solomon it was Wisdom (Sophia) who led Israel through the wilderness and slaked her thirst by providing water from the flinty rock (11:1-4). Philo identified this rock as Wisdom,[60] a personified attribute of God by which the transcendent and distant God was involved as guide and protector of Israel. Since for Paul, Christ is the Wisdom of God (I Cor. 1:24), it is not extraordinary that he would in reciting the legend simply conclude, "And the Rock was Christ."

The force of Paul's argument as he warns one group on the basis of the experiences of another is dependent upon the degree to which he can demonstrate the similarity of the situations of the two communities. To the common experiences of baptism and the communion meal Paul added this third which encompassed all the other aspects of the analogy: both Israel and the Corinthian church had experienced "Christ."

The form of this affirmation of the pre-existence of Christ is obviously quite different from those previously noted which were structured upon the descent-ascent pattern and also quite different from those which united mythical time (pre-creation) and historical time (redemption). Here the idea of pre-existence is framed horizontally, not vertically, upon a

---

[59] *Tosefta Sukka* III, 11, 12.
[60] *Leg. Alleg.* II, 21.

timeline totally within observable history. This passage asserts that previous to that epiphany which lies at the center of the church's proclamation, the Christ was at work among "our fathers."

As strange as this may seem to a modern reader whose mind has been conditioned to receive empirically grounded data, this perspective is neither foreign nor unreasonable to the faith and orientation of the early Christian community. While there were some in the early church, such as Marcion, who felt that the preservation of the identity and purity of Christianity necessitated the removal of all evidences of Judaism, the main body of the faith accented the church's continuity rather than discontinuity with Israel. Jesus Christ came not to destroy but to fulfill; all who believe on God in Jesus Christ are Israelites, children of Abraham according to faith; the patriarchs of Israel all died looking to the Christian age as the fulfillment of that story of which their lives were earlier chapters; Christianity is the very substance of that which Judaism foreshadows; the God who has spoken in a Son had spoken before in various ways and in various degrees to the fathers through the prophets.[61] These and countless other expressions throughout the New Testament bear witness to the fact that the Christians saw in their experience of God's love and purpose in Jesus Christ continuity with the experiences of that love and purpose among the people of faith in times past. What Christians perceived in Jesus was of

---

[61] These reflections are primarily from Hebrews, but the fact that the church kept the OT in her Bible is another witness to this sense of continuity.

the same nature as that which the fathers in faith had come to see as the heart of Judaism, behind all the trappings of worship and fine print of regulations. God seeks and enters into redemptive covenants with men. He has now come to us in Jesus of Nazareth, but he is the God who is always coming.[62] It is not surprising, therefore, to read from an early Christian writer: "The prophets who prophesied of the grace that was to be yours searched and inquired about this salvation; they inquired what person or time was indicated by the *Spirit of Christ* within them when predicting the sufferings of Christ and the subsequent glory" (I Peter 1:10-11). Or again, from another: "By faith Moses . . . considered abuse suffered for *the Christ* greater wealth than the treasures of Egypt, for he looked to the reward" (Hebrews 11:24*a*, 26). And the literary vehicles as well as the theological categories lay at hand to express this continuity of past and present in the history of salvation. Earlier Hellenistic Judaism had shown that her deposit of truth in the Law of Moses was really the concretization of Wisdom, pre-existent and therefore not bound to any one time or place.[63] Later Christian apologists were to appeal to the best pagan minds by saying that the truth expressed in Christ was the embodiment of the Logos, the Word or reason, pre-existent and therefore not bound to time or place but sought always and everywhere by

---

[62] More clearly pointed up in the form of the Christian confession which says "The Christ is Jesus." In this order, the expectation (Christ) is expressed prior to the fulfillment (Jesus).

[63] Ecclus. 24.

lovers of truth.[64] Likewise in this passage Paul has used a view of Christ as pre-existent and therefore not confined to Jesus of Nazareth.[65] Paul here employed this methodology to warn an arrogant group within the church that they should profit by the errors of the community of faith of ancient times. Remember, urged Paul, Israel fell in spite of the fact that she had drunk from the supernatural rock, "and the Rock was Christ."

This third and final Pauline variation of the category of pre-existence functions to unite, as did the other two. As the doctrine of a pre-existent Christ had elsewhere served to join creation and redemption, essence and existence, so here it serves to unite past and present in the apparently discontinuous history of the Jewish and Christian churches.

Pre-existence in the Fourth Gospel. Consideration of pre-existence in this book will necessarily involve the entire work rather than specific passages, as was the case with Paul. Unlike Paul's letters, addressed to specific questions and congregational difficulties, the Fourth Gospel is a theological treatise, carefully constructed on discernible premises concerning God, Christ, and the world, and with unifying themes consistently

---

[64] Justin Martyr and Clement of Alexandria made this approach to Greek intellectuals.

[65] Whether Paul believed in a pre-existent "Christ" before he believed in Jesus is, of course, an open question. We lack a knowledge of the nature of his pre-Christian Judaism. The issue has been discussed again by Schoeps, *Paul,* pp. 23 ff.

recurring throughout the book.[66] Those who argue that the Prologue (1:1-18) is not really related to the remainder of the work apparently do so on two grounds. First, the literary form of these verses seems to be that of a poem or hymn to the Logos, adapted and modified with parenthetical references to John the Baptist.[67] The English reader can discern this literary quality by reading the passage as a unit, omitting verses 6-8 and 15. However, if it is a hymn incorporated by the writer, its portrayal of Christ and of the world is characteristic of the entire book. Second, it is only in the Prologue that the term Logos or Word is used in reference to the Christ. And yet, as will be noticed repeatedly, that which is conveyed by this term is conveyed in other ways in practically every sign and discourse related by this evangelist.

Therefore, the essential Christology of this Gospel, with its affirmation of Christ's pre-existence, is given to the reader at the outset.

In the beginning was the Word, and the Word was with God, and the Word was God. He was in the beginning with God; all things were made through him, and without him was not anything made that was made. . . . And the Word became flesh and dwelt

---

[66] The best presentation of the overall approach and message of the Fourth Gospel is found in Bultmann, *Theology of the New Testament*, II, 3-92.

[67] For a study of the literary form of the Prologue, cf. Jeremias, *The Central Message of the New Testament* (New York: Scribner, 1965), pp. 71-90. Also Bultmann, "Der religionsgeschichtliche Hintergrund des Prologs zum Johannes-Evangelium," *Eucharisterion* (Festschrift für Hermann Gunkel; Göttingen: Vandenhoeck & Ruprecht, 1923), pp. 5 ff. Bultmann and Jeremias hold opposite positions on the relation of John the Baptist to the origin of the Prologue.

among us, full of grace and truth; we have beheld his glory, glory
as of the only Son from the Father. . . . No one has ever seen
God; the only Son, who is in the bosom of the Father, he has made
him known. (1:1-3, 14, 18)

In this Gospel the writer has put the burden upon the
reader to listen, to hear and accept the Word of God which
is not simply a spoken Word but the eternal Word now incarnate in Jesus of Nazareth.

Those who first read this Gospel obviously were more able
than moderns to grasp the imagery used here. Many cultures
and religions in that world had traditions and myths about
a divine Word, all of which were set in a profound respect
for the nature and power of a word.[68] Those who are ac-
customed to expressions such as "Talk is cheap," "It isn't what
you say that matters," or "Words will never harm me," can
hardly appreciate the ancient man's view of a spoken word
as an expression of one's self, a part of one's essence or being
released into the world. As such, a word had identity and
power, almost as though it were an entity separate from the
one who said it. This word could bless or curse, heal or wound,
liberate or enslave. Thus among the Israelites God's Word
always accomplished its mission; it never returned empty.[69]
God spoke the world into existence: "By faith we understand
that the world was created by the word of God, so that what
is seen was made out of things which do not appear" (Heb.

---

[68] See chapter I for examples from Hellenistic philosophy and religion.

[69] Ps. 33:4-7 is an example of the treatment of the Word of God as an
entity with power in itself. Also Isa. 55:10-11.

11:3). In chapter I it was observed that in the forms of Judaism which sought to make the ancient faith attractive to the best Greek minds, there was a concept of Wisdom (Sophia), often used interchangeably with Word (Logos). All men sought this Wisdom which had been expressed both in creation and in history, but her dwelling place was in the tents of Jacob. Philo had spoken of the Logos as an intermediary between God and the creation, between God and man. The Stoic philosophers spoke of Logos or reason as the pervading and unifying principle in all things, including man. Their distinction between the indwelling (*endiathetos*) Word in the mind of man and the expressed (*prophorikos*) Word, spoken or sent out from man, provided later church fathers a philosophical structure upon which to discuss how Christ as the Word could be divine and eternal, separate and distinct from God, and still not a violation of the basic oneness of God. A number of Hellenistic religions, with varying degrees of kinship with Gnosticism, had myths of a being named Logos who served as a mediator between God and the world in matters of creation and revelation. The portrayal of the Logos in the Fourth Gospel as a divine being or person seems to indicate closer affinity with the language and imagery of these Hellenistic religions than with the philosophical idea of an all-pervading Reason.[70] However, the definition of

---

[70] I have preferred the mythological understanding of the Logos to the philosophical as more appropriate to the portrayal of the Logos in this Gospel. For this and other debates relative to the affinities in this Gospel with Judaism and Hellenism, cf. C. H. Dodd, *Historical Tradition in the Fourth Gospel* (Cambridge: Cambridge University Press, 1963); C. K. Barrett, *The Gospel*

the idea in the Gospel of John is not necessarily determined by any particular source, even if such were known, but from the function of the idea in the writer's purpose.

This Gospel, like all meaningful religious discourse, addresses the problem of man and his situation in the world. The world, including man, is not essentially dark and evil, for it is God's creation through the instrumentality of the Word. In fact, the possibility of any ultimate dualism which explains reality in terms of two sources, one good and one evil, is eliminated at the outset. "All things [the totality] were made through him, and without him was not anything made that was made." Therefore, the darkness that is in the world is due not to the world's dark nature or dark source but to man's choice to turn away from the light; men "loved darkness rather than light" (3:19). Men turn from the Creator and find their center, their home, in the visible, transient, created, relative values.[71] This absolutizing of relative values is to live according to this world; it is to judge by appearance and not by truth (7:24). In this condition men become proud, secure in their value systems and institutions, and will preserve the *status quo* at all costs, even murder. Thus it became "expedient" that Jesus should die (11:50). This worldliness assumes its ugliest shapes in the entrenchments of religion, barricaded in robes, temple, tradition, regulation, and ritual, blessing every gross error with a proper text and re-

---

According to St. John (New York: Seabury, 1960); Bultmann, *Das Evangelium des Johannes* (Meyer's *Kommentar;* Göttingen: Vanderhoeck & Ruprecht, 1962).

[71] Bultmann, *Theology of the New Testament*, II, 15 ff.

sisting at every step the Word of God. Even if a man has been crippled for thirty-eight years (ch. 5) or blind from birth (ch. 9), still he cannot be healed today; it is the sabbath and the rule is of more value than the man. Jesus cannot speak the truth because "he has never studied" (7:15). Jesus cannot be the Christ; he is from the wrong section of the country. "Search and you will see that no prophet is to rise from Galilee" (7:52). Even the words of the Bible hinder the Word. "You search the scriptures, because you think that in them you have eternal life; and it is they that bear witness to me; yet you refuse to come to me that you may have life" (5:39-40). Illustrations from this Gospel of such perversion of means into ends, such worldliness with clean-washed face and folded hands, could be multiplied, but these suffice to point out that the world has alienated itself from God. In this state of separation men are bound in darkness (8:12; 12:35), in sin (8:32-34), in falsehood (8:43-45; 17:17), and in death (5:24; 11:25).[72]

Into this world the Word came. Two most important truths must be understood about this Word. First, it is the same Word which was mediator of the world's creation and which is the world's life and light (1:3-4, 9). The Redeemer is Creator; the Creator is Redeemer. Second, this Word came from God, from above, from outside the created order; it is pre-existent. As such, even though he "dwelt among us" (11:4), and even though he was embodied in Jesus of Nazareth who had a mother and brothers; who grew weary, hun-

---

[72] *Ibid.*

gry, and thirsty; who wept, bled, and died; still this Word is noncontingent. The Word incarnate in Jesus spoke and acted always and purely from the vertical relation to God, never from the horizontal interchanges of mutuality and social influence. The Word is from "above," not "of the earth"; "in the world," but not "of the world." He acted at the feast in Cana according to his "hour" to reveal his glory, not at his mother's bidding (2:1-11). He fed the five thousand, not (as in the Synoptics) as a response to a need that arose, but in the context of a larger purpose, "for he himself knew what he would do" (6:6). He went up to Jerusalem to the Feast of Tabernacles not because his brothers urged him, but because of reasons that transcended the historical circumstances (7:1-10).[73]

At no point does the "from above" nature of the ministry of the incarnate Word appear more clearly than in the Lazarus story. Martha and Mary send word to Jesus: "Lord, he whom you love is ill" (11:3). Most surprisingly, this word which would have brought running even the most insensitive was thus received: "Now Jesus loved Martha and her sister and Lazarus. So when he heard that he was ill, he stayed two days longer in the place where he was" (11:5-6). How strange and how apparently without feeling! It is, however, necessary to observe that the sisters spoke of the one "loved" with the word *filia*, a word for love that denotes friendship, mutuality, love on the horizontal of human relationship. But

---

[73] The writer distinguishes between chronological time and "his time" (J. E. Bruns, "The Use of Time in the Fourth Gospel," *NTS*, XIII [1967], 285-89).

Jesus, because he "loved," tarried. The word here is *agape*, the love with which God loves, the love "from above." [74] What does this strange exchange say of the Word? Just as the incarnate Word did not act at his mother's bidding, or at his brothers', so here he did not act at the prompting of friends but "from beyond" the contingencies of every human situation. The author goes so far in accenting the noncontingent nature of the Word that the one in whom that Word is incarnate seems nonhuman, or inhuman. [75] The Lazarus story was but the shadow of the real substance of the Gospel: the death and exaltation of the Son (11:4). [76]

That the Word came from outside to address the world is amply illustrated also in the inability of those addressed to comprehend the Word. For the Christ and for those who heard him the same words had entirely different meanings. The Samaritan woman welcomed the word about living water with hope of never having to come back to the well to draw (4:15). Nicodemus was puzzled over the biological difficulties of being born again (3:4). The Jews could not envision the constructural possibility of rebuilding in three days a temple which took forty-six years to erect (2:19-20). The disciples wondered who brought Jesus his lunch when, upon their return from Sychar where they had bought food, Jesus said,

---

[74] I think W. F. Howard (*Interpreter's Bible*, VIII, 806-7) is in error in seeing no difference here and in ch. 21 in the two words for love. There is too much at stake to say the two words are interchangeable.

[75] Note 11:36. The fact that the *Jews* say Jesus wept because he loved (*filia*) Lazarus is clear evidence that John intends to say that is *not* the reason.

[76] W. F. Howard, *Interpreter's Bible*, VIII, 648-50.

"I have food to eat of which you do not know" (4:32). To Jesus' statement about going away to his Father the Jews responded with questions about his traveling abroad among Gentiles (7:35-36). These and many other such occasions of confused meanings declare dramatically that the Word was not of the world. The world, dull of hearing, translated the Word into its own value system, thereby missing its power to effect both judgment and grace. However, those who did perceive and receive the Word passed from death to life; for them the crisis of judgment had passed (3:36; 5:24).

In accord with this portrayal of Jesus as the incarnate Word, Jesus was crucified, but he was no victim. His life was not taken but given (10:18), for he knew that he came from God and that he would return to God (13:3). The Heavenly Revealer's earthly sojourn was over, and he asked to be restored to the glory that had formerly been his (17:5). The death of Jesus, rather than being here presented as vicarious or atoning for sin,[77] was a glorification (12:23; 13:31), for by means of it the pre-existent one returned home.

In this context what is the meaning of pre-existence? Quite evidently the category is used to mean precreational, with both temporal and spatial connotations: temporal in that the Word was previous to creation, and spatial in that he came from outside, apart from the cosmos. But pre-existence does not thus serve to give the reader an avenue of escape into a

---

[77] Although John the Baptist heralded him as "the Lamb of God, who takes away the sin of the world" (1:29), Jesus dies not as a lamb slain for sin but as the Passover Lamb (19:31-37).

time and place outside this present world. On the contrary, pre-existence provides the category for addressing the world in judgment and in grace. The world is judged because the Word which came as Revealer-Redeemer is the selfsame Word by which the world was created. In view of its origin, therefore, the fact that the world needs this redemption is the sharpest judgment. Pursue the same thought in reverse and the other half of the truth becomes clear: the world is addressed in grace because the same Word which created it has now come to it, speaking to the world from within it in Jesus Christ. No higher view of creation, no greater "compliment" to the world can be framed than the incarnation. No more adequate view of redemption exists than that which describes it as the restoration and fulfillment of creation. This Gospel has no room for anticosmical dualism, no place for world-negating attitudes. With pre-existence as the larger frame of reference, the author is able beautifully and dramatically to structure the paradox by which the world has her hope: he is not *of* the world and therefore *can* redeem; he is *in* the world and therefore *will*.[78]

Pre-existence in the Epistle to the Hebrews. Even though an earlier reference was made to a statement in Hebrews concerning the pre-existence of Christ (11:26), that single reference in no way properly represents the writer's principal

---

[78] The preservation of this paradox will become a crucial issue in the next chapter in the current debate over the possibility of preserving the transcendent in modern theology.

use of pre-existence in his portrayal of Christ, especially in the first two chapters. Here there is no reason to deal with passages in isolation because this theological treatise is a unit, and the portrayal of the Christ as pre-existent, even though expressed several times in a number of ways, is a whole, consistent within itself and with the message of the book.[79] It would be advantageous to get these expressions in mind in advance of any consideration of the author's purpose and his particular accent upon pre-existence.

In many and various ways God spoke of old to our fathers by the prophets; but in these last days he has spoken to us by a Son, whom he appointed the heir of all things, through whom also he created the world. He reflects the glory of God and bears the very stamp of his nature, upholding the universe by his word of power. When he had made purification for sins, he sat down at the right hand of the Majesty on high, having become as much superior to angels as the name he has obtained is more excellent than theirs. (1:1-4)

In these opening lines the entire theme of his Christology is given by the author: the Son pre-existed with the Father, reflecting the very nature and character of God; the Son was God's mediator in his relationship with the world, in creation and in continued sustenance; the Son was God's mediator in the work of redemption; the Son now sits exalted on the right

---

[79] For a discussion of introductory matters, cf. Feine-Behm-Kümmel, *Introduction to the New Testament*, p. 273, and the standard commentaries, esp. Otto Michel, *Der Brief an die Hebräer* (Meyer's *Kommentar;* Göttingen: Vandenhoeck & Ruprecht, 1960), pp. 1-33.

hand of God. In the elaboration of his argument various aspects of this Christology receive accent. Christ as Creator receives attention in 1:10: "Thou, Lord, didst found the earth in the beginning, and the heavens are the work of thy hands." Christ as Redeemer is presented in a messianic interpretation of Psalm 8, by which the writer interpreted the humanity of Jesus as a significant chapter in the Son's work, for he was "for a little while lower than the angels" (2:7).[80] And finally, Christ as exalted Lord at God's right hand is repeatedly emphasized. Note: "Thy throne, O God [referring to the Son], is for ever and ever" (1:8); "Sit at my right hand, till I make thy enemies a stool for thy feet" (1:13); or again, "Thou hast crowned him with glory and honor, putting everything in subjection under his feet" (2:7*b*-8).[81]

The intensity of the writer, his conscious effort to persuade, his succession of arguments as though in debate, force the reader of this letter to back off in order to grasp its purpose, to see its governing consideration. The Epistle to the Hebrews is not really an epistle but a speech, a sermon, a word of exhortation designed to demonstrate the superiority and the adequacy of the Christian faith, most probably to a church that had become discouraged, disappointed, and perhaps frightened by persecutors (2:3; 3:12; 4:1, 11; 5:11–6:8; 10:32-39; 12:1-4). This the author seeks to accomplish by

---

[80] The Septuagint, not the Hebrew text, is quoted. The "while" is significant, making the humiliation of Christ temporary.

[81] This exaltation theme is central to Hebrews since the most significant ministry of the Christ takes place after his exaltation as intercessor before God in our behalf (7:25).

drawing contrasts. These contrasts are not designed solely to underline the discontinuities between Christianity and Judaism. Rather, he seeks to show that the Christian faith is the fulfillment of that which Judaism foreshadowed, the end toward which Israel moved (11:39-40).

It is apparent, however, that the form of Judaism reflected here, or at least the interpretation given Judaism, is not what is usually referred to as normative rabbinic Judaism. The structures upon which the author framed his exposition, both of the nature of Judaism and Christianity, are philosophical. The opening paragraph in praise of the Son is so strikingly similar to the praise of Sophia in Wisdom of Solomon (7: 25-27) that literary kinship is unquestionable.[82] The Platonic categories of pre-existence and existence, the real world of the idea or form and its material, earthly shadow or reflection, are obvious throughout the argument. This is evident not only in specific statements—"For since the law has but a *shadow* of the good things to come instead of the true *form* of these realities, it can never, by the same sacrifices which are continually offered year after year, make perfect those who draw near" (10:1)—but in the entire argument as to the superiority of Christianity over Judaism.[83]

Assuming the reader was familiar with and accepted the category of the physical as the visible, unreal shadow of the

---

[82] But the literary kinship does not justify interpreting Hebrews by Wis. of Sol. Hebrews addresses quite a different problem. Purpose, not source, is the major determinant of definition. For literary kinship, cf. J. M. Robinson, "A Formal Analysis of Col. 1:15-20," *JBL*, LXXVI (1957), 270-87.

[83] A. C. Purdy, *Interpreter's Bible*, XI, 585.

essence, the author carefully demonstrated that tabernacle, priests, sacrifices, promised land, sabbath rest, Mt. Sinai, and all other elements of Judaism were shadows of the real. For example, the Jewish priests "serve a copy and shadow of the heavenly sanctuary; for when Moses was about to erect the tent, he was instructed by God, saying, 'See that you make everything according to the pattern which was shown you on the mountain' " (8:5). This pattern is the Christian faith; it is of the essence, the body (*soma*) not the shadow (*skia*). Faith for this writer, therefore, is that capacity to live in the world of the physical and transient, yet to lay hold of the eternal and true, and by the certainty of that apprehension orient one's entire life. Ample illustrations of those who thus lived by the unseen are cited from the history of Israel (ch. 11).[84]

In man's quest for meaning and salvation it was, of course, believed to be essential that he have contact with and be related to the metaphysical realm, for here the essence of life was to be found. In this quest angels and other spirit beings which were beyond the limitations of the physical world and which were seen as intermediaries between God and man came to occupy a central place. Just as the development in heterodox Judaism of the belief that the Law was given by angels[85] came to be a serious threat to the Mosaic tradition,[86] so the

---

[84] Heb. 11 is a striking parallel to the recitation of Israel's history in Wis. of Sol. where wisdom, not faith, leads the men of God.

[85] Heb. 2:2; Acts 7:35, 53; Gal. 3:19.

[86] Louis Ginzberg, *Eine unbekannte jüdische Sekte* (New York: Selbstverlag des Verfassers, 1922).

worship and adoration of angels came to be for Christianity, at least in some quarters, an attack upon the primacy and the adequacy of Jesus Christ.[87] Gal. 3:19-4:11 and Col. 2:8-19 reflect essentially the same problem, as was noted earlier in this chapter.

Therefore, strange and irrelevant as it may seem to a modern reader, the author felt it necessary to address the problem of angels at the very beginning of his treatise. With an admirable combination of logic and scriptural references he said: God never called an angel Son (1:5); the angels are specifically commanded to worship the Son (1:6); the angels, quite unlike the Son, are changeable according to the service being rendered, being at times wind, at other times fire (1:7-8); the angels are servants in a universe that is transitory (1:11-12); the angels are not invited to sit on God's right hand (1:13); not to angels has the world to come been subjected (2:5); angels are not even the objects of God's plan of redemption (2:16); and while the angels were the transmitters of the Law, here in the Son is a superior message (2:2-4).

The author realized, however, that the vulnerable point of his argument lay in the known fact that Jesus Christ suffered in ways common to men, that he was tempted as all men are, and that he took his place in mankind's solemn procession to the grave. How could one who suffered the humiliation and apparent defeat of death be superior to angels who transcend this creaturely condition?

---

[87] I fail to see how A. C. Purdy (*Interpreter's Bible*, XI, 603) can say there is no polemic against angel adoration here.

In two sweeping arguments the writer attacks this stumbling block to faith in Jesus Christ. In the first place, in order to redeem man it was fitting that the one who would lead man back to God be like man.

Since therefore the children share in flesh and blood, he himself likewise partook of the same nature, that through death he might destroy him who has the power of death, that is, the devil, and deliver all those who through fear of death were subject to lifelong bondage. For surely it is not with angels that he is concerned but with the descendants of Abraham. Therefore he had to be made like his brethren in every respect, so that he might become a merciful and faithful high priest in the service of God, to make expiation for the sins of the people. For because he himself has suffered and been tempted, he is able to help those who are tempted. (2:14-18)

Rather than close his eyes to the earthly career of Jesus Christ, this author argues as strongly as any New Testament writer for the humanity of the Christ, a humanity complete in order that he might completely redeem "his brethren."

However, the second line of his argument in response to those who questioned the adequacy of the redemptive power of one who suffered and died was to set the earthly career of Jesus into the larger context of the eternal. Admittedly, Jesus was, in his humanity, lower than the angels (Ps. 8), yet his humiliation was but a brief episode in the larger scheme of God's purpose. "Thou didst make him *for a little while* lower than the angels" (2:7). Here the author interpreted Psalm 8 messianically. He built his argument upon the Septuagint rather than the Hebrew text, because the phrase in Hebrew translated "a little lower than God" in the Septuagint may be translated "for a little while lower than the angels." The expression "for a little while," therefore, set the humanity of Jesus between the pre-existent glory of the Son through whom and by whom all things exist (1:2-3) and the exalted glory of the Son crowned with glory and honor, having all things subject to him (2:7-9).

The motif for this Christology is the descent and ascent of the Savior,[88] a pattern now familiar through earlier examinations of II Cor. 8:9, Phil. 2:6-11, and Col. 1:15-20. The pre-existent became existent, the metaphysical became physical in order that he might lead "many sons to glory" (2:10). This treatment of the pre-existence of the Son is in a number of ways strikingly similar to the Christology of Col. 1:15-20. Both address a troublesome form of Judaism; both seek to correct angel worship; both affirm the Son as mediator both of creation and of redemption; both include angels among the creatures who are subjected under the lordship of Christ; both understand the arena of redemption to be history.

It is at this last point, however, that this writer expanded upon that which was but briefly stated in Colossians. In Colossians the act of redemption in history is the death on the cross; this is the reconciling event. The cross is the point in time that serves to unite the entire drama of God's purpose from pre-existence to ultimate restoration of all things visible and invisible. In Hebrews the death of Christ is stressed both as a redeeming event and as the necessary preliminary to

---

[88] But not to the extent that the line of Jesus' history is reduced to a point.

Christ's entering into God's presence to abide as a continuing intercessor and high priest for his people (7:25). However, the earthly career of Jesus is not presented as a single event, the cross, as in Colossians, but in a larger frame including temptations, suffering, constant devotion to God, obedience, and death.[89]

> In the days of his flesh, Jesus offered up prayers and supplications, with loud cries and tears, to him who was able to save him from death, and he was heard for his godly fear. Although he was a Son, he learned obedience through what he suffered. (5:7-8)

Christ was "one who in every respect has been tempted as we are, yet without sinning" (4:15*b*).

Pre-existence for this writer, therefore, serves as the larger context that frees him to explain and to present fully the fact of Jesus' humanity and humility. He felt no necessity, on the one hand, to protect Jesus from humanity or, on the other, to offer frequent reminders that the Son was *really* suffering the contingencies of existence. With pre-existence in the background, the writer had a context for understanding Jesus Christ and the "for a little while" nature of his life. Because the Son is pre-existent and eternal, his sharing with his flesh and blood brethren is more than a sympathetic but futile leap into our pit; he is *able* to redeem, to accomplish the work of salvation. Without this larger frame of

---

[89] Paul's apparent interest in only the "that" of Christ's life and death (Bultmann, *Theology of the New Testament*, I, 293) is not enough for this writer.

reference the life and ministry of Jesus would appear a dismal failure indeed,[90] and men would wisely seek the help of angels to attain life and fulfillment. But he who suffered and died is pre-existent. By this the author means precreational, both in the sense of being prior to and involved in the creative process and of having priority over all that has been created, both men and angels.

Pre-existence in the Apocalypse. If for the writer of Hebrews it was Jesus' own suffering and death that demanded a larger context for grasping its theological significance and relation to creation, for the author of the Apocalypse it is the suffering and death of the Christians themselves.

Apparently the churches of Asia Minor faced at the time of this writing a severe persecution from Rome.[91] The author has already heard in the distance the columns marching down upon the Christians, bringing suffering (Rev. 2:10), imprisonment (2:11), and death (7:14). For this tribulation the churches were unprepared, being torn by heresy (2:6, 14, 20; 3:9), weakened by indifference (2:4; 3:15), immorality (2:14; 3:4), and materialism (3:17). The seer wrote to reprove, to warn, and to comfort.

As at other times when the people of God suffered at the hands of unbelievers, when hope appeared nowhere on the

---

[90] Some modern writers such as Paul M. van Buren do not need this larger frame of reference to see meaning in Jesus' ministry. See the next chapter for discussion and evaluation.

[91] See Martin Rist's "Introduction to Revelation," *Interpreter's Bible*, XII, 347-65.

horizon, when the chariots of mass cruelty trampled into the dust the hopes of the faithful community, the Word from God came in apocalyptic form.[92] The visionary lifted his eyes from the bloody pages of current history and saw the great war of which the current persecution was but a battle. The war was, in the ultimate sense, between God and Satan. The tide of the battle in Asia Minor was apparently in the enemy's favor; the church was suffering at the hands of her enemies. However, in the larger perspective of the war between God and Satan the current persecution of Christians is seen as but a momentary victory by the force that will finally be defeated.

It was, of course, some real encouragement to the readers to remember that Jesus himself was martyred by these unbelievers, but God had exalted him. In fact, the Lamb is now on the throne (5:6, 12-13). Those who, like Jesus, stand firm and faithful to the end will also be vindicated in the final triumph of good over evil.

The stronger encouragement, however, came in the very nature of apocalyptic writing. The writer, with benefit of vision, took a position above history in order to see the meaning in its movement and its finale. He spoke to the fundamental question raised by people who are forced to endure prolonged distress and undeserved privation, those tortures of mind and body known only to those who are victims at the hands of the unscrupulous and unbelieving. The question is inevitable: What meaning does this experience have in the

---

[92] See the discussion of I Enoch in chapter I.

context of the purposes of God? In critical times men ask the ultimate questions, breaking through the no-longer-cozy framework of here and now to demand answers at the door of ultimate reality. As was noted in the previous chapter in the brief sketch of the book of Enoch, the apocalyptic perspective arises out of that life situation in which history is no longer home and men look beyond the physical to the metaphysical.[93] In this crisis the writer drew back the curtain which separates the discoverable processes of history from the invisible and eternal verities. The readers were permitted to see Christ transcending the whole sweep of human history and to hear him speak as the Alpha and the Omega, the first and the last, the beginning and the end (1:17; 22:13).

The expression "the Alpha and the Omega" does not in itself specify pre-existence, but it is apparent that pre-existence is here involved.[94] This formula is used to speak of God himself (1:8; 4:8; 21:6) who created all things (4:11) and of Christ who is the beginning of God's creation (3:14).[95] Herein lies a motif basic to the message of the book: as in the beginning when created order came out of

---

[93] Apocalypticism and Gnosticism grow out of the same historical conditions, but differ due to the difference in the theological background of those who suffer at the hands of history. R. M. Grant tends to forget this difference in his view of Gnosticism growing out of apocalypticism (*Gnosticism and Early Christianity*).

[94] For a discussion of these letters as they relate to speculations on the divine name, cf. Austin Farrer, *The Rebirth of Images* (London: Dacre, 1949), pp. 261 ff.

[95] C. F. Burney's article is almost too imaginative but does explore the richness of the expression "Beginning of Creation" ("Christ as the ΑΡΧΗ of Creation," *JTS*, XXVII [1926], 160-77).

chaos, so out of the chaos and struggle of this world there is to be a new creation, a new heaven and a new earth (21:1). Just as Christ was the beginning of the first creation, he is the beginning of the new creation.

The emphasis upon pre-existence in the Fourth Gospel and in Hebrews was also seen as precreational, but here the striking difference is due to the nature of apocalyptic imagery. In the Apocalypse, which addresses those who suffer the exigencies of painful history, the orientation is almost totally toward the eschaton, the end time, and the "beyond history" consummation of the divine justice. The beginning is not nearly as important as the end; it is not so much a question of "whence" as it is "whither." The reference to the beginning and pre-existence is present, however, to grant assurance as to the end. He who was involved in the first creation will be effective in the victory over evil which is necessary to the new creation. He conquered primeval chaos; he can and will therefore conquer historical chaos. The Omega of history is both defined and guaranteed by the Alpha, for the Christ who is both Alpha and Omega is pre-existent, standing outside and above the victimizing forces of chaos and evil.

The early Christians knew well enough that the powers of evil had put to death Jesus of Nazareth, the incarnation of the pre-existent Son. But they were not to be downcast, for they also knew that this was a part of the divine strategy for victory, "wrought in the stillness of God." So wrote Ignatius, Bishop of Antioch early in the second century. As a prisoner of Rome approaching martyrdom, Ignatius addressed words of confidence to the Christians at Ephesus, one of the churches addressed in the Apocalypse.

How then was he manifested to the world? A star shone in heaven beyond all the stars, and its light was unspeakable, and its newness caused astonishment, and all the other stars, with the sun and moon, gathered in chorus round this star, and it far exceeded them all in its light; and there was perplexity, whence came this new thing, so unlike them. By this all magic was dissolved and every bond of wickedness vanished away, ignorance was removed, and the old kingdom was destroyed, for God was manifest as man for the "newness" of eternal life, and that which had been prepared by God received its beginning. Hence all things were disturbed, because the abolition of death was being planned.[96]

Summary. This survey of the meanings of pre-existence in New Testament materials has been based upon three presuppositions: the category of pre-existence already lay at hand in the intellectual and religious milieu; the meaning of the idea for a New Testament writer is not necessarily the same as the meaning of the idea in background materials; and the meaning of pre-existence for one New Testament writer is not necessarily the same as for another. In fact, Paul used pre-existence with entirely different accents within the same letter to the Corinthian church. In other words, definitions

---

[96] Letter to the Ephesians, 19, in *The Apostolic Fathers*, trans. Kirsopp Lake (Loeb Classical Library; Cambridge: Harvard University Press, 1952), Vol. I.

have been arrived at functionally, determined by the use of the idea in the service of the writer's purpose.

To say that function has been the primary canon for understanding affirmations of the pre-existence of Christ is not, however, to say that Christology, or theology in general, is to be viewed with a utilitarian eye. This study has insisted all along that "functional" and "utilitarian" are different. That difference may appear to be one of degree, and any issue that hinges upon a difference of degree is a most delicate one. A functional Christology is one which is framed to address the immediate needs and questions of the hearers. Unless, however, the concern for relevance be balanced and disciplined by a concern for the truth claims of that which is presented, then a functional approach may degenerate into utilitarianism.

Herein lies a central question raised by this study, a question crucial for the whole field of religious discourse. To what extent does the human situation influence and determine the Christian proclamation? The church is concerned that her message be true, that it correspond to reality, and yet she is also concerned that her message be relevant to the human predicament. The church has always tolerated theological "purists" and theological "practitioners" because both are essential to her life. She will not sacrifice truth on the altar of relevance, nor vice versa. This is the major issue in current theological discussion: What is the nature and extent of the modification of Christian affirmations in order that they speak meaningfully to culture? To this issue much of the next chapter will be addressed, and therefore the conclusions of this chapter will be framed in anticipation of that discussion. This is not to sacrifice the New Testament study to a current concern; this is precisely the concern with which the New Testament writers struggled.

It was observed in chapter I that in a variety of ways the category of pre-existence served men who were experiencing a sharp sense of discontinuity with existence in their world. This loss of at-homeness, this sense of insecurity and alienation from one's situation in life, was created by a variety of factors: breakdown of political structures, popularization of belief in demonic powers and principalities controlling human affairs, astrological speculations, prolonged persecution and privation, and man's own awareness of himself as transcending the promptings of nature and the circumstances of his existence. Pre-existence, therefore, characterized the essence; the eternal, noncontingent realities which are prior to the parentheses of birth and death, creation and consummation. Pre-existence provided a ground of security for the insecure by presenting certainty back of the present uncertainties,[97] by offering a characterization of what was the nature of things before the tragic story of existence began. When man understood his problem to be existence, he viewed a knowledge of the pre-existent as both comforting and redemptive, if coupled with information as to how life could return to that pre-existent state.

---

[97] This is not to say pre-existence owes its life in the Christian faith to the fact that it helps meet man's need for security. It also relates to the continuing quest for the truth about reality: how is the ontic to be perceived?

Against this background of uses of pre-existence the early church shaped its affirmations of the pre-existence of Christ. As far as the New Testament is concerned, the writers apparently felt free to modify the Christological statements to address the particular conditions and problems of the readers. If the problem was the material universe, then the portrayal of Christ as pre-existent was essentially that of a redeemer who was precreational. If the problem was angels and principalities, then Christ was pre-existent in the sense of being prior to the angels and being the one by whom they exist. If the problem was history, then Christ pre-existed in that he was prior to, and hence not himself a victim of, history. If the problem was an apparent lack of meaningful continuity within history, then Christ pre-existed in the sense of transcending the structures of time and place, being available to all men past and present.

But if this observation is correct, how does the Christian proclamation stop short of total capitulation to culture? How does the Christian faith prevent being only an echo, simply a restatement of the problems so that questions sound like answers? Or expressed from another perspective, if there is always a close correspondence between man's predicament and God's self-disclosure,[98] is it not possible that there is no disclosure at all: man is simply responding to himself?[99]

---

[98] The terminology here is from Lewis Sherrill's adaptation of Tillich's method of correlation (*The Gift of Power* [New York: Macmillan, 1955], chs. 4-5).

[99] Which is, of course, autonomous humanism.

What we have seen in these New Testament materials (and it is true of the whole history of Christian doctrine) is the adapting of what was adopted from the culture. The tradition is kept alive by redaction. And why redact? Why not keep the tradition pure and unalterable? Because man and his needs are not foreign to the gospel; they are part of it. The gospel is not a completed drama, fixed and to be used only in recitation; the audience is part of the cast. The Word of God is in its very nature a communicated Word. It is a moot question to ask about the *unheard* Word of God. And if the Word of God is the Word of God *heard*, it is heard by men with categories and terms into which that Word is to be cast if it is to be appropriated.

Is this, then, a modification only on the level of language? Definitely not. There is no such thing as modification *only* on the level of language. Language is much too complex and meaningful for such to be the case.[100] This is amply illustrated in two obvious stages of modification of tradition in the early Christian appropriation of the Old Testament. The first modification was already made and available for the church: the Septuagint. The Septuagint was more than a translation from Hebrew to Greek; it was an interpretation and a modification of the Hebrew tradition.[101] The second modification was made by the church. With a strong Christology as the governing consideration, the Greek text of the

---

[100] Recall Wolfson's error with Philo (chapter I, n. 15).

[101] As the use of Ps. 8 in Heb. 2 illustrates.

Old Testament yielded many "proofs" of the truth of the Christian message.[102]

If the Christian community so modified its tradition from Judaism, it is reasonable to assume it modified its own traditions[103] as the church faced new problems in its mission to the nations. In fact, in I Corinthians the reader is permitted to see the modification of tradition in process (chs. 7, 11, 15). Also in Col. 1:15-20 there may be evidence that a body of material was (1) taken over from Hellenistic religion, (2) adapted for a baptismal liturgy, and (3) as it now stands, recast into a polemic against the Colossian heretics.[104]

It is not always possible, nor is it the present purpose, to identify strata of tradition with subsequent redactions within the New Testament.[105] Apparently some of the confusion in the Pauline churches was created by the existence within those churches of differing traditions or differing modifications of the tradition he had delivered.[106] For example, the Corinthians may have supported their dualistic understanding of reality by an appeal to Gen. 1-2, as mediated through

---

[102] For example, for Matthew's doctrine of the Virgin Birth, the Greek *parthenos* was essential.

[103] Birger Gerhardsson overlooks the NT itself in his view of an airtight, catechetical transmission of the tradition from Jerusalem (*Memory and Manuscript*, trans. Eric Sharpe [Uppsala: University Press, 1961]).

[104] So argues Ernst Käsemann, in "A Primitive Christian Baptismal Liturgy," trans. W. J. Montague, *Essays on New Testament Themes* (Studies in Biblical Theology, No. 41; Naperville: A. R. Allenson, 1964, pp. 149 ff.).

[105] For a good example of such a study, cf. A. M. Hunter, *Paul and His Predecessors* (rev. ed.; Philadelphia: Westminster, 1961).

[106] I Cor. 15:1 ff. Paul "traditioned" what "had been traditioned" to him.

Philo.[107] Of course, Paul's understanding of creation led him to reject all world-denying dualism.

It was apparently under the pressure of such problems, of such magnitude as to threaten a shift of the community from its Christological center,[108] that certain modifications were made in the Christian proclamation. This flexibility, this willingness of the church to make modifications in its Christological affirmations, seems to veer very close to concession and capitulation to culture. And yet this very flexibility most likely saved the church from that certain death which comes from being ignored by a culture that quits listening because it hears nothing meaningful.

But again the question arises: What limits were there to this modification of the tradition? What prevented an eventual loss of the tradition, an evaporation of the gospel? In the New Testament affirmations of the pre-existence of Christ reviewed in this chapter certain limitations to the appropriation of traditions from the culture (whether Jewish or Hellenistic) and the modification of earlier Christian tradition are evident.

First, the ascription of pre-existence is not to all men, but reserved for Christ alone. Certainly the category of pre-existence came to Christology from anthropology. This fact gave the category much of its meaning for the Christian proclamation, for it provided a way to affirm the Savior's identification with the pilgrimage of man. To adopt this mode of

---

[107] See chapter I, n. 17. I Cor. 10:1-4 indicates both Paul and the Corinthians may have known Philo.

[108] See Samuel Laeuchli, *The Language of Faith* (Nashville: Abingdon, 1962).

thinking for presenting the Christ while at the same time denying it for man in general admittedly created a problem, especially for later efforts to systematize Christian doctrine.[109] However, the alternative was totally unacceptable. The New Testament writers insisted man is, body and spirit, a creature of God and in God's image. His existence is a created existence and it is good, not evil. Man need not seek, therefore, to find himself through a myth of pre-existence. Man does have a problem but it is not existence; it is sin. No creature but only a creator, or a mediator of creation, would in this understanding be pre-existent.

A second limitation is a close corollary of the first: the pre-existent Christ is both Creator and Redeemer. For him to be only one or the other would be opening the door to dualism and the possible erosion of the foundation of the faith, monotheism. The Redeemer is not, therefore, seeking to redeem man from the Creator of this world. On the contrary, the Redeemer is the Creator; the Creator is Redeemer.

A third limitation to the modification of Christology is a further extension of the first two. Because Christianity affirms history as meaningful, the cyclical view of life with its perspective of pre-existence, existence, and return had to be broken. The Christian faith insists that the line of history, which is the arena where God works and makes himself known, has intersected this cycle with the joyful proclama-

---

[109] Origen, for example (*De Principiis*, Bk. I, ch. 3), felt the consistency of his system demanded the pre-existence of human souls, a position later to be branded, of course, as heresy.

tion that at a point and place in time the meaning of life, the very heart and nature of ultimate reality, has been revealed. Eternity has moved into time; God has come seeking man in man's own context of created and contingent existence. The incarnation is God's high compliment to the creation and to history. Redemption is within history; the kingdom of God is in our midst. For all the uses the church made of the category of pre-existence as a means of speaking of the truly Real, the finally and ultimately Meaningful, these were never permitted to obscure the "in history" dimension of her gospel. This, in fact, was the unique and almost incredible force of the Christian message in contrast to other religions that claimed the favors and blessings of countless divine beings: Christianity announced that men have been sought, found, and addressed in human life.

When the New Testament writers adopted from the culture a hymn or poem in praise of a pre-existent being and employed it as a motif for expressing their own Christology, they were careful to insert "by the blood of his cross," or "even death on a cross," or "became flesh," or "flesh and blood like his brethren." In later creedal formulas the historical accent was preserved with insistence: "suffered under Pontius Pilate" and "crucified, dead, and buried." The oldest known eucharistic liturgy begins quite historically, "On the night in which he was betrayed" (I Cor. 11:23). The church of a later generation wisely insisted that the Christian Bible include the Old Testament to testify to the historical context and continuity in which Christianity shares. And the specifically Christian portion of the Bible begins with a genealogy, fol-

149

lowed by a record of the life and work of Jesus of Nazareth in Galilee. The language of pre-existence is not left to sail in ethereal realms as metaphysical poetry; the New Testament inserts the prose of crib and cross.

But even with these limited modifications of appropriated terms and modes of thinking, the modern reader feels himself not at home with the thought world of the New Testament. Affirmations of the pre-existence of Christ, although adapted and recast along the lines suggested, still seem foreign to our age.

Throughout this study traditional language has deliberately been employed with the awareness that the reader would feel the distance between himself and the pages of the New Testament. Is the distance of such a nature that it can be negotiated by linguistic changes and translations of the ideas into contemporary vocabulary? There is no question but that much could be done on the level of language to increase understanding of the Christian proclamation. But perhaps the problem is a deeper one, calling into question the mythological and metaphysical presuppositions upon which all the affirmations of Christ's pre-existence are structured. It is one matter to say the task before the church is to clarify in order to communicate meaningfully her proclamation of the pre-existent Christ. It is an entirely different matter to say the task of the church is to question the truth claim of that proclamation.

To the discussion of this crucial issue we turn now in the final chapter.

(3)

Meanings Past and Present

This study has insisted that the function of the category for a writer is the primary canon for understanding New Testament affirmations of the pre-existence of Christ. This course has been followed in full awareness of the dangers of utilitarianism, a trap into which theology falls when the concern to be relevant is not balanced by a concern to speak the truth. This investigation has led to the conclusion that, at least with reference to the dimension of pre-existence, the New Testament presents a functional Christology.[1] Whether

---

[1] Cullmann has insisted NT Christological titles referring to pre-existence are functional, not essential (*Christology*, pp. 3-5, 247). R. H. Fuller feels this view is generally correct but needs modifying at the points where the NT reflects Christologies of the Hellenistic Gentile mission (*Foundations of New Testament Christology*, pp. 248-49). For Roman Catholic reactions to Cullmann, cf. L. Malevez's article "Functional Christology in the New Testament," *A Theology Reader*, ed. R. W. Gleason (New York: Macmillan, 1966), pp. 133 ff.

the functional approach meant that Christology was "always a variable" [2] remains to be seen.

The functional nature of New Testament Christologies does mean that faith and culture were always in dynamic interrelationship. To express faith the Christian community had to have a store of available and appropriate concepts and modes of thought. To be sure, the church proclaimed the Word of God, but it is equally true that her word was a human word revealing her participation in the hopes and anguish of her time.[3] One does not discover, therefore, in the New Testament that the culture was being censured for erroneous science, medicine, or psychology, as though the church had, by revelation, a more advanced understanding of the universe.[4] The language used in communicating the gospel was indigenous to the context of the hearers and the speakers.

In view of this approach to understanding the New Testament materials, the reader may with good reason find the title of this chapter a contradiction of that approach. How could one presume to comment on what the pre-existence of Christ meant in the first-century context if that meaning was

---

[2] H. Braun, "Der Sinn der neutestamentlichen Christologie," *ZTK*, LIV (1957), 368.

[3] See the concise but clear discussion of this point by W. A. Luijpen in *Phenomenology and Humanism* (Pittsburgh: Duquesne University Press, 1966), pp. 133-37.

[4] Whenever the church sees herself as the revealer of hidden reality, she is threatened by the attitude of a Galileo. Cf. John Wren-Lewis, "Does Science Destroy Belief?" *Faith, Fact, Fantasy*, ed. C. F. D. Moule *et al.* (Philadelphia: Westminster, 1964), pp. 18 ff.

worked out in a dialogue between the Christian missionary and the human condition he addressed, a dialogue in which we did not participate? In the introduction to this study, methods for understanding New Testament materials that stood outside the materials were rejected. Must not this present attempt and the attempts of all commentators and interpreters of the proclamation of others likewise be rejected?

In the light of several recent theologies of the Word of God, this would seem to be the case. According to this perspective the Word of God is to be understood primarily as *address,* not as *meaning.* Therefore one listens and decides as to his response; interpreting that Word is out of order as an evasive maneuver.[5] One who proclaims the gospel has his thinking informed by the gospel tradition, to be sure, but if there is a real occurrence of the Word, it must come to expression in each context in language shaped by that context. Each situation is unique. There may be little or no observable continuity with the gospel tradition, or with that same person's proclamations of the gospel in other contexts.[6] If the proclamation is therefore to be understood only as *address,* then it would be a sterile exercise, to say the least, to interpret that proclamation from a geographical and chronological distance.

Without question, this understanding of the Word of God

---

[5] R. W. Funk, *Language, Hermeneutic, and Word of God* (New York: Harper, 1966), pp. 16-17.

[6] R. W. Funk, "The Hermeneutical Problem and Historical Criticism," *The New Hermeneutic,* ed. J. M. Robinson and John B. Cobb, Jr. (New Frontiers in Theology, Vol. II; New York: Harper, 1964), p. 170.

is refreshing and humbling: refreshing in that it saves the Word from being reduced to a discussion without involvement, humbling in that it breaks the arrogance often accompanying masterful commentary upon scripture. However, to view the proclamation of the Christian faith as *address* only is inadequate at two points. First, it is an inadequate portrayal of the nature of the Scriptures as the primary records of the proclamation. The varieties of form and content,[7] shaped by a variety of functions to which the material was put (worship, polemics, evangelism, catechism, etc.), simply defy a single category or a single characterization.[8] Second, presenting the proclamation only as address is too limited in the nature of the listener's response. The address asks the listener to decide to obey or not to obey, but the listener rightly insists that his decision is both prior to and subsequent to understanding. He asks for *meaning,* not as one who seeks to avoid decision, but rather as one who must find meaning simply because he is a human being.[9] The offer of meaning is also intrinsic to the proclamation.

It is not, therefore, contrary to the nature of the materials before us to attempt to find the meaning of the pre-existence of Christ in those materials. It would be contrary to the method of this study to seek to find that meaning by searching for an irreducible core in the Christological affirmations

---

[7] Funk's work has thus far been on the parable and the epistle. Cf. *Language, Hermeneutic, and Word of God.*

[8] Amos Wilder, *The Language of the Gospel* (New York: Harper, 1964).

[9] Amos Wilder ("The Word as Address and as Meaning," *The New Hermeneutic,* pp. 198-218) cogently argues this point.

that have been examined. Such a core, provided it could be located, would be an extraction, a residue after the distillation of all variables, and would not itself represent the proclamation in any real situation.

We ask the writers, therefore, how they understood the pre-existence of Christ. Wherein lay the principal significance of this mode of thinking? Once this question has been faced, it will likely be our discovery that we are well on the way to understanding what meaning, if any, the pre-existence of Christ has for our time.[10]

Meanings Past. The language of the New Testament about Jesus Christ is homological.[11] Christology is by its very nature confessional, and all the language about Christ that is apparently descriptive is in the service of confession. A transcendental interpretation of him grew out of the encounter of men with Jesus. Whether or not pre-existence was employed to convey that interpretation was dependent in part upon how the ontic was perceived by the persons addressed. The fact that some New Testament writers[12] do not present a pre-existent Christ does not mean that they did not have a transcendental interpretation of him. As we have observed, for Hellenistic culture historical existence was practically useless as a category for conveying meaning. Such was not the case with the mainstream of Judaism. With its fundamental

---

[10] Wilder, *Language of the Gospel,* p. 131.

[11] Gerhard Ebeling, *Theology and Proclamation,* trans. John Riches (Philadelphia: Fortress, 1966), p. 82.

[12] The Synoptic Gospels, Acts, the Pastorals (excepting the quotation in I Tim. 3:16), and most of the Catholic Epistles.

doctrines of monotheism and creation, historical existence could and did serve as the arena for encountering, and as the category for expressing, transcendence. The mythological and metaphysical presuppositions necessary to the Hellenistic Christian proclamation are therefore absent from the earliest Christian preaching in the context of Judaism.[18] Current "rediscoveries" of Jesus by writers who have no appetite for metaphysics erroneously use these early affirmations if they interpret the absence of pre-existence as signifying that the New Testament writers involved were transcendentally neutral.

The story the Christians told was the story of an event in history, but theirs was never a concern merely for history. The event of Jesus Christ was revelational. The usual biographical interests in family background, education, work, associations, cause of death, etc., were viewed and so were related, if related at all, as revelatory. In Jesus Christ, God was revealed. For Judaism this meant, of course, the chastened, corrected, and fulfilled messianism, promised by the God who comes, the God of Abraham, Isaac, and Jacob. For Greeks, however, that which was revealed was the Essence, the Unconditional under the conditions of existence, the Eternal in time. With all the rich variety in the New Testament Christological affirmations, there is through it all a common factor: the message about Jesus was presented in such a way as to permit the Essence, the Ultimate, God, to be seen in and

---

[18] Palestinian Judaism, even though the discovery of the Dead Sea Scrolls has rendered invalid the broad distinctions once made between Palestinian and Hellenistic Judaism.

through the account of a saying or an event. After all, the interest in Jesus was precisely this: What was *God* saying or doing here?

The New Testament writers differ from each other in the degree or intensity of the accent upon the presence or activity of God in Jesus or upon the Essence evident in his existence. In the Synoptic Gospels at a number of points the story is so concerned to present the "existential" struggle of Jesus of Nazareth that the Eternal or God stands in the shadows or does not appear at all. Jesus' temptation and the Gethsemane experiences are cases in point.[14] In the Fourth Gospel, however, the writer's purpose, shaped by the problems he had to address, was to remind the readers in every paragraph that while the figure before them was Jesus of Nazareth, he was actually the embodiment of the divine, unconditional, pre-existent Logos. So whenever Jesus speaks, it is from above; it is the eternal Word. The man Jesus of Nazareth is therefore obscured or blurred in the writer's expressed and consistently pursued business of confronting the reader with the ultimate reality. Jesus of Nazareth is the vehicle for the Word, but as a real human being in himself, he is never clearly in focus. Genuine human existence is almost sacrificed in the descriptions of pre-existence or essence. "He who has seen me has seen the Father" (John 14:9).

The New Testament writers also differ in the manner in

---

[14] Yet even here it must be admitted that the reader is aware of God and of the resurrection triumph as he reads these stories. Otherwise these Gospels would not have been written; in fact, they would not have been "Gospels." The "messianic secret" was a secret perhaps to Jesus' immediate audiences but not to us.

which the metaphysical or essential dimension of the story is related to the historical or existential. The Synoptic Gospels record the story within the bounds of historical existence; that is, between the birth (the baptism in Mark) and death (and resurrection) of Jesus. However, every event is told in such a way as to make the reader conscious of the pre- and postexistent dimensions of the story. The portrayals of Jesus teaching, healing, doing mighty works, are drawn so as to impress clearly upon the reader that Jesus is not simply "of Nazareth"; he can be understood only in the context of eternity.[15]

Outside the Gospels the entire history of Jesus is most usually capsuled in a single phrase: "descended from David according to the flesh" (Rom. 1:3); "born of woman, born under the law" (Gal. 4:4); "he became poor" (II Cor. 8:9); "making peace by the blood of his cross" (Col. 1:20); "manifested in the flesh" (I Tim. 3:16); "in the days of his flesh" (Heb. 5:7); "for a little while lower than the angels" (Heb. 2:8). Of course, such reduction of the historical to a single point, simply affirming that he was an event in history, allows no room for speaking of the metahistorical *within* the historical as do the Gospels.[16] Rather than telling the story of Jesus

---

[15] The experience of reading the Synoptics' portrayal of Jesus is somewhat analogous to looking at a sheet of paper on which is written "historical existence" while on the back side of the paper and bleeding through is the expression "metaphysical pre-existence." Reading the Gospel of John would be analogous to the same process with the paper reversed.

[16] Cf. Bultmann's discussion of the NT's mixture of language about myth and history (*Kerygma and Myth*, ed. H. W. Bartsch, trans. R. W. Fuller [Torchbooks; New York: Harper, 1961], p. 34).

with the transcendent "shining through" each saying or each event, the brief statement of Jesus' historicity is set in the context of eternity. The fact of his existence is the middle of a three-chapter "history": pre-existence, existence, postexistence or exaltation.[17] The Christological hymn in Phil. 2:6-11 is a clear example of this. By thus framing the Christological affirmation the writer conveys the element of transcendence or the metaphysical dimension by separating it from the historical. The "pre-" and "post-" framework in which the historical data about Jesus is set makes the reader aware that the historical has ultimate significance.

These two ways of handling the word of faith concerning Jesus as the event of "God with us" accomplish the same result, and both fulfill the writers' purpose. They and the Christian communities of which they were members saw in Jesus what God was doing for man. Had they not believed this, they would have had no reason to tell the story. As it is, even those forms of the message in which the transcendent seems most subdued are as shouts from the housetop, "that you might believe."

It is no wonder, therefore, that the material about Jesus Christ in the New Testament has continually frustrated "objective" historians who have sought the facts about Jesus apart from the faith of the writers. In fact, many Christians, seeking to have their faith legitimized by historical accuracy, chased down dead-end streets questions such as "What *really*

---

[17] For a clear discussion of this point, cf. J. M. Robinson, *A New Quest of the Historical Jesus* (London: SCM Press, 1959), pp. 50-52.

happened?" or "What was Jesus really like, uninterpreted?" The quest for the historical Jesus is not futile, of course, but many questions remain questions, especially to one whose devotion to objectivity forces him to stand outside the circle of faith, to screen critically every report by Jesus' followers, and to be satisfied with no less than stenographic reports and photographs. The clear fact remains: the church has never witnessed to his existence without the interpretation of that existence. This is not less true of those who do not explicitly use the category of pre-existence to convey the element of the transcendent and metahistorical than of those who do.[18]

Interestingly enough, some of the strongest accents upon the human, finite, conditioned life of Jesus are to be found in those New Testament writers who separate the metahistorical and historical, the pre-existent and existent, phases of the Christ event. Having made the reader aware of the transcendent origin and destiny of the Christ, usually by means of the descent-ascent formula, the writers are free to make vividly real the contingent and conditioned history of Jesus of Nazareth. The Fourth Gospel does not betray its basic thesis when Jesus is portrayed washing and drying the feet of fishermen because the writer has set this vignette in the larger context of Jesus' knowing "that he had come from God and was going to God" (John 13:3). Paul's Christ is in human form, obedient, and suffers death, but the reader sees this picture hanging between two others: one in which Christ is

---

[18] Even in the "old quest" for the historical Jesus, the transcendent came through the portrayals of Jesus, though often in romanticism and sentimentalism.

in the form of God on equality with God, and the other in which the exalted Christ is declared Lord of heaven, earth, and hades (Phil. 2:6-11). The writer of the Epistle to the Hebrews, because he is confident that Christ is the pre-existent agent of creation and the very image of God's character, is completely free to speak of the tears, fears, sufferings, temptations, and obedience of Jesus (Heb. 1:2-4; 2:5-18; 4:14–5:8).

It is important to understand, however, that this reduction of the historical data about Jesus Christ to a single point, such as birth or ancestry or death, is in no sense a sacrifice of history. It is not as though these writers were mentioning somewhat apologetically this "chapter" in the eternal story but not relating it meaningfully to the whole. It was exactly this sacrifice made by the Gnostics within the church which made them "heretics." They lost their perspective, accenting the metaphysical, the supernatural, with a negation of historical existence. As is true of most heresy, it was a loss of balance, a distortion of truth.[19] In this process of radical dehistoricization the Christian faith dissolved into a myth, and in its later stages Gnosticism degenerated into a cosmological science. The Christology of Gnosticism was not strong enough to subordinate and reinterpret cosmology; cosmological speculation controlled the center of interest, and into that grand myth Christ was fitted.

In the New Testament the historical event of Jesus, wheth-

---

[19] See the excellent discussion of this point by Samuel Laeuchli in *The Language of Faith.*

161

er elaborately or briefly told, is never told as a dark interlude, a tragic interruption in the grand pilgrimage of the Son, a narrow vale between God and God which, for some strange reason, had to be tolerated. On the contrary, all the meaning about the essential and ultimately real nature of life which the category of pre-existence conveys is found, realized, and expressed within this historical existence.

On the other hand, this is not to say that the New Testament preserves the historical fact of Jesus Christ as though it thereby proved the reality and certainty of the gospel and legitimized the faith.[20] Verifiable historical objectivity as a canon by which to weigh value and meaning is not found in the New Testament but is brought to it by the modern reader. Rather, the New Testament preserves the historical center of its gospel because it is thereby saying something about the ultimate significance not only of Jesus Christ, but of all history, and of our history in particular. The history of Jesus Christ puts all historical existence in a new light, elevating it as the realm of God's activity and of man's discovery and fulfillment of his true nature.[21]

It is for this reason that the "highest" Christologies are not designed to imply that the pre-existent Son only pretended to

---

[20] This error of the older quest for the historical Jesus the new quest seeks to avoid. Whether or not it does is debated (Van Harvey and Schubert Ogden, "How New Is the 'New Quest of the Historical Jesus'?" *The Historical Jesus and the Kerygmatic Christ,* ed. Carl Braaten and Roy Harrisville [Nashville: Abingdon, 1964], pp. 197-242).

[21] For Paul there is no alternative between Christology and anthropology. Christology is anthropologically drawn. On this matter, cf. Hans Conzelmann, "Paulus und die Weisheit," *NTS,* XII (1966), 244.

be a man, as though there were something essentially and
unalterably wrong with being a man, a station to which no
self-respecting divinity could stoop. The negative orientation
toward life which is capsuled in the popular expression "We're
only human" renders impossible any truly serious apprecia-
tion for the gospel of the incarnation or any honest acceptance of the New Testament declaration of the significance
of the here-and-now. Thoughts here run on a two-way street.
On the one hand, an acceptance of the possibilities of genuine
human existence is pre-requisite to acceptance of the word of
the gospel about the historical existence of Jesus Christ. To
deny the former makes it necessary to deny he really existed
or to say, in effect, that he was playing the role of a human
being. On the other hand, it is the real and genuine historical
existence of Jesus Christ that opens up the possibilities of this
life for each person.

It is not surprising, therefore, that in the New Testament
the affirmations about Christ are interwoven with affirmations
about the experiences common to the lives of those addressed.
The story of Jesus Christ is not told as a self-contained drama
that took place "out there" or "back there" from which we
draw lessons and meanings for our existence.[22] It is not structured on a two-point outline, the first a presentation of what
he was and did and the second an application of what we are
to be and do. As man's story is clarified by the event of Jesus
Christ which brings it to light, so the event of Jesus Christ is

---

[22] Günther Bornkamm, "Myth and Gospel," *Kerygma and History,* ed. Carl
Braaten and Roy Harrisville (Nashville: Abingdon, 1962), pp. 172-96.

understood only when it is involved with the lostness and the redemption of man. Three examples from the New Testament will help clarify this characteristic of Christological statements.

The writer of the Epistle to the Hebrews, because he structured his Christology upon the pre-existence–existence–exaltation pattern, had a perfect opportunity to minimize if not totally erase the historical existence of Jesus in favor of the grander themes of his doxology to Christ. Such is not the case, however. Christ is an efficacious redeemer not in spite of, but because of, what he endured (Heb. 2). He learned obedience and was perfected through what he suffered. His life, one of tears and temptations, is meaningful and fulfilling for us because it was so for him. In and through the contingencies of existence, in and through the life currents that are summed up in the word "history," the essence of life and the nature of reality are known.[23]

One might expect that the Fourth Gospel, accenting as it does the divine, creative Word incarnate in Jesus, would look upon the death of Jesus as a necessary pain on the threshold of joy in being restored to pre-existent glory. That is, the death of Jesus could be considered the release of the pre-existent Logos which had been confined in Jesus. But this is far from the truth as the writer of this Gospel understands it. The cross is not a prelude to glorification, but the cross *is*

---

[23] E. C. Colwell reminds us that we are not to use our understanding of God to interpret Jesus, but rather our understanding of Jesus to create a view of God (*Jesus and the Gospel* [New York: Oxford University Press, 1963], p. 49).

the glorification of the Son (11:4; 12:23). In this Gospel Jesus interprets his approaching death with two analogies: in the realm of nature, it is in dying that a seed bears fruit; in the realm of discipleship, it is life lost in humble service that is life truely and fully. "And what shall I say? 'Father, save me from this hour?' No, for this purpose I have come to this hour." (12:27.) This is the same dramatic denunciation of the idea that man is to escape this life for a better world as is found in the account of the footwashing at the last supper. "You also should do as I have done to you" (13:15). There is no other way to know God than through obedient service. "If any man's will is to do his will, he shall know whether the teaching is from God" (7:17). The Eternal is known and is manifested in and through humiliation and service, not through speculation on the pre-existent order of things. That this is true is revealed in the life of him who did not come to do his own will but the will of God. Free from the necessity of preserving his own life, he was thus able to make known the essence of life itself.

Some of the clearest illustrations of a transcendent Christ being seen through the lens of common human experience are to be found in Paul. All that Paul sought to signify by the categories of pre- and postexistence, he did by relating these dimensions to the one very historical fact: the cross (Phil. 2:8; Col. 1:20). The cross rather than being an embarrassing admission was the center of Paul's message, for the humiliation and death of Jesus opened up for Paul the nature of life's meaning and the very intention and ultimate purpose of creation. Toward this, pre-existence and creation pointed; by this, the consummation of all things received its definition and its guarantee. This event, located and dated in history, interpreted the great cycle of eternity and reconciled all things in heaven and on earth (Col. 1:20; Phil. 2:10-11). Paul's own appropriation in faith of the Christ event produced in him not speculation about the pre-existent but an identification with Christ in his suffering (Col. 1:24-25; Phil. 3:10; Gal. 6:17). Paul's own suffering illumined his Christology; Paul's Christology illumined his own suffering.

This interweaving of Christology and human experience, each to a certain extent clarifying the other, was not for Paul limited to reflection upon Christ's suffering and upon his own suffering for Christ's sake, but included the experiences of the whole church. The life and worship of the church was for Paul an actualization of Christology, and the clearest witness to the meaning of the incarnation of the pre-existent one was a sincere Christian life in the community of faith. The two most elaborate hymns to the pre-existent Christ to be found in Paul are employed to urge the Philippians and Colossians to actualize in ethical steadfastness the meaning of being "in Christ." Cosmological categories that had served others before him to explain man's situation in the world Paul employed to explain Christ, and Christ explained man. In the language and terms of that day Paul explained Christ existentially, and he explained existence Christologically.[24] Christology and anthropology are inextricably interwoven themes. In fact, in some passages in Paul it is difficult to ascertain

---

[24] Bornkamm, "Myth and Gospel," p. 196.

whether the principal subject is the reader and his experience or Christ and his redemption. Each serves as commentary upon the other.

Even a casual reading of Col. 2:8-15 will bear out the truth of this observation concerning Paul's Christology.

See to it that no one makes a prey of you by philosophy and empty deceit, according to human tradition, according to the elemental spirits of the universe, and not according to Christ. For in him the whole fulness of deity dwells bodily, and you have come to fulness of life in him, who is the head of all rule and authority. In him also you were circumcized with a circumcision made without hands, by putting off the body of flesh in the circumcision of Christ; and you were buried with him in baptism, in which you were also raised with him through faith in the working of God, who raised him from the dead. And you, who were dead in trespasses and the uncircumcision of your flesh, God made alive together with him, having forgiven us all our trespasses, having canceled the bond which stood against us with its legal demands; this he set aside, nailing it to the cross. He disarmed the principalities and powers and made public example of them, triumphing over them in him.

Is the principal topic here the experience of the Colossians or the lordship of Christ over all powers? Both, for they are one great whole. With shuttle-like movements Paul speaks of the fullness and freedom of the Christian life, and yet he expresses the same theme from another perspective when proclaiming Christ's triumph over the enslaving powers. The Colossians' death to sin is made possible by the death of

Christ; the death of Christ is certified and clarified by the Colossians' death to sin. Baptism draws upon the death of Christ for its meaning; the death of Christ is made meaningful in the experience of baptism.[25]

All this is to say that for Paul, Christology cannot be divorced from the historical context and experiences of the believer. Gnosticism (radical dehistoricization) effected this divorce and made Christology a cosmic drama of a pre-existent being. Humanism (radical historicization) effected this divorce, reduced theology to anthropology, and denied that historical existence participated in any transcendent meaning. Both errors bless their conclusions with a Pauline text. This is unfair to him. While it is true Paul has no Christology divorced from anthropology, no tradition which does not insist upon the *ante me* and *extra me* dimensions of Christology is accurately Pauline. That Paul's thought centered in Christ prevented degeneration into an anthropocentric circle; that his thought centered in Christ crucified prevented degeneration into cosmological speculations about the pre-existent.

Had the early church permitted the category of pre-existence to move to the controlling center of its Christology, obliterating the historical and existential dimensions, it is quite likely that it would have, as a corollary development, embraced the doctrine of the pre-existence of the human soul. This would have been a natural consequence, and such

---

[25] The same interweaving of Christology and Christian experience is found in Eph. 5:22-33.

an affirmation about both Christ and man in general would have been a clear announcement that the basic problem of man is his creatureliness, his historically conditioned existence. A gospel for such a predicament would have involved an initiation into the mysteries of pre-existence and a summons to ecstatic trances and world-denying asceticism. But, said Paul, the Christian faith denies this. Christ touches us here and now, and he does so as an agent of creation and redemption in the midst of human affairs and relationships.

What, then, is man's basic problem? Paul insisted it is sin, but not in the sense of an isolated conflict with God. Rather, man's problem is sin in the sense that man shares in the alienation, distortion, and hostility in the universe. Man needs to be reconciled to his Creator so that he can again see himself and his world as creatures and to accept this as God's gift rather than either pretending that created values are absolutes to which to anchor life or evils to be denied and avoided. Since the entire cosmos is involved in this error, reconciliation must be cosmic; there can be no private or partial redemption. Such is the nature and scope of the redemption in Christ who "made peace by the blood of his cross" (Col. 1:20).[26]

Whatever other meanings it held for Paul, the cross for him declared as inadequate any systems that made sharp distinctions between essence and existence, for here in one historical event was revealed the essence of existence.[27] And this

---

[26] Fully presented by A. D. Galloway in *The Cosmic Christ* (New York: Harper, 1951).

[27] The Ephesian letter declares that in the cross all barriers between earth and heaven and between Jew and Gentile have been broken down.

event was, and is, continually being certified in the lives of believers who have died and have been raised with Christ, and who manifest the same in the homes and communities where they live.

The affirmations of the pre-existence of Christ forged in the mission of Hellenistic Christianity reveal the capacity of the early church to be relevant but not utilitarian. Relevance demanded of the church an adaptation of her message about Christ to categories already meaningful and available within the culture. However, the conviction of the church about the truth claims of her message led her to demand of the hearers a radical modification of their understanding of the meaning of history. Not to have made the first modification would have meant irrelevance; not to have insisted on the second would have meant capitulation.

The wisdom of this course was approved and canonized at Nicea and Chalcedon.

Meanings Present. With unprecedented honesty, the contemporary church is engaged in a radical re-examination of the content of her faith. The topics central to this critical reassessment are the traditional Christian doctrines of God and of Jesus Christ. There is very strong "existential" reaction against the "essential" language of Chalcedon, Nicea, and the New Testament,[28] language still recited in a church that

---

[28] R. H. Fuller (*Foundations of New Testament Christology*, p. 248) is quite correct in seeing the ontological questions already being raised in the NT in the literature from the Gentile mission.

no longer thinks or finds meaning in ancient modes such as pre-existence. The culture of the Western world has been totally saturated with the spirit of scientific inquiry and verification. The supersensory and metaphysical world to which the category of pre-existence belongs is necessarily rejected by science as a methodological procedure. Such a world is simply not available as an object for investigation.[29]

Whether it be cause for lament or celebration, the fact is obvious: the world has become secularized. Man no longer feels the need for the metaphysical to understand the world or to function within it.[30] "Man has learned to cope with all questions of importance without recourse to God as a working hypothesis."[31] As anti-Christian as this may seem at first, the fact remains: the church helped toward this process of secularization. The Christian faith de-divinized the world, worked to destroy the belief that the world was hostile and alien to the human spirit, and affected the freedom of man to be master and not victim of the world.[32] Secularization may therefore be understood as the fulfillment of the Judeo-Christian tradition.[33]

But with what result for Christology? Does secularization mean that transcendence is necessarily eliminated as a mean-

---

[29] Bultmann, "The Idea of God and Modern Man," trans. R. W. Funk, in *Translating Theology into the Modern Age* (New York: Harper, 1965), pp. 84-85.

[30] Harvey Cox, *The Secular City* (New York: Macmillan, 1965), pp. 2-3.

[31] Bonhoeffer, *Prisoner for God: Letters and Papers from Prison*, ed. E. Bethge, trans. R. H. Fuller (New York: Macmillan, 1959), p. 145.

[32] Bultmann, "The Idea of God and Modern Man," p. 86.

[33] This is the thesis of Cox in *The Secular City*.

ingful dimension of the Christian proclamation? The issue does not touch Christology alone; it is a question of whether we can talk of God at all in an age that has abandoned the traditional metaphysical view of reality for a strictly historical view.[34] The mainstream of theological discussion coming out of Europe in recent years has been focused, not upon God, but upon the Word of God. The expression "of God" should perhaps be in parentheses because of the hesitation of these theologians to speak of God. Remaining metaphysically neutral, discussions center upon the event of the Word.[35] In such an atmosphere is there actually any meaning to the New Testament affirmation of the pre-existence of Christ?

Obviously, the church has been guilty of Christological anachronism, tending to identify what is said with the way it is said. Preservation of the faith has been synonymous with preservation of certain terms and categories. Words that opened doors and windows of understanding centuries ago today shut out light, and the summons to faith is obstructed by obscure language. The church agreed long ago that Gentiles did not have to become Jews in order to become Christians. So now it has to be determined that citizens of our world do not have to become citizens of the Graeco-Roman world in order to be Christians.

There is, therefore, much health in the current reaction against the categories of some New Testament Christologies.

---

[34] Ebeling, *Theology and Proclamation*, pp. 15 ff.

[35] Primarily the work of Ernst Fuchs and Gerhard Ebeling in Germany and R. W. Funk in this country. For a survey of the positions of all three, cf. Funk, *Language, Hermeneutic, and Word of God.*

The new concern for historical existence serves to break down the docetic Christology that arose from a distorted preoccupation with pre-existence and essentialistic thinking. This new orientation also serves to shatter the social and political indifference which infected the church during the time of her "metaphysical captivity." Now one can again hear in the churches invitations to Christian discipleship that involve decisions amid contingencies rather than calls to hide in insulating absolutes.

This is to say that in terms of the language in which the gospel is communicated the church has made and is making hurried but helpful strides toward addressing modern man. The Christian community is making a variety of responses to the disastrous fact that for many, faith had become simply "appropriating the incredible." [36]

Roman Catholic theology, though by no means unanimous, has tended generally to reaffirm Chalcedonian Christology as a legitimate and necessary evolution beyond the New Testament. This reaffirmation regards existential and functional Christologies as violations of the truth claims of the gospel entrusted to the church. The Christian understanding of the person of Christ is grounded in revelation, and apart from this understanding no salvation remains.[37] Some Protestant scholars agree that modern listeners to the Christian proclamation stumble at Chalcedon but not at the New Testament.

---

[36] Ebeling, *Theology and Proclamation*, p. 18.

[37] Cf. Malevez, "Functional Christology in the New Testament," and *Word and Redeemer*, ed. J. M. Carmody and T. B. Clarke (Glen Rock, N.J.: Paulist Press, 1966), pp. 126 ff.

This position recognizes that in the New Testament, Christological titles stating or implying pre-existence are functional rather than essential.[38] This re-examination of New Testament categories, and especially the reaffirmation of the church's heritage in Judaism with its nonmetaphysical orientation, goes far toward satisfying the contemporary preference for language about God's activity over against language about ontic reality.[39] However, lest the matter be oversimplified, it should be remembered that developments toward an ontology are also to be found in the New Testament in those documents which come from the Gentile mission.[40] With reference to these documents in which affirmations of Christ's pre-existence are set in language "irretrievably katabatic," [41] many feel that the church can reinterpret the "katabasis" mythology without tossing it out as obsolete baggage.[42]

Of course, most of the current efforts to interpret and translate New Testament Christology so as to confront this generation with the gospel are indebted to the pioneer work of Bultmann.[43] No one has shown more sensitivity to modern man's need nor more concern to reach him with the gospel of Christ. Bultmann's existential interpretation of the gospel has necessarily raised the question of the pre-existence of Christ:

---

[38] Cullmann, *Christology*, pp. 3-5.

[39] H. W. Montefiore, "Towards a Christology for Today," *Soundings*, ed. A. R. Vidler (Cambridge: Cambridge University Press, 1962), p. 151.

[40] Fuller, *Foundations of New Testament Christology* (cf. n. 28 above).

[41] *Ibid.*, p. 255.

[42] *Ibid.*, p. 256.

[43] Especially his programmatic essay of 1941 (*Kerygma and Myth*, pp. 1-44).

how is it to be understood today? In a recent interview Bultmann repeated with exceptional clarity his understanding of
this Christological affirmation.

Interviewer: Jesus Christ as the "only-begotten son of God"
—does this demand of Christians that they believe in the pre-
existence of Jesus, that he was a heavenly being who came down to
earth? If not, what does "pre-existence" mean, demythologized?

Bultmann: In the Pauline passages about the pre-existence of
Jesus Christ, what is expressed is that the person and destiny of
Jesus do not have their source and significance within a context of
worldly occurrences but that God has acted in them.

Interviewer: Could not, must not—when you so formulate it
—even many a conservative theologian agree with you?

Bultmann: Let me put it this way: It is a fact that there is a
proclamation, authorized by God himself, of his prevenient grace
and love. This fact finds its mythological expression in the talk
about the pre-existence of Christ.[44]

However one may evaluate Bultmann's program of interpretation, it is vital to notice that in his hands Christology is
not reduced to anthropology.[45] As Bultmann understands
the gospel, man stands before God, and authentic life depends
upon his being confronted with the gospel of Jesus Christ, the
proclamation of God's act which is *ante me* and *extra me*.
The dimension of transcendence is undeniably present.

---

[44] "An Interview with Rudolf Bultmann," *Christianity and Crisis*, XXVI,
(1966-67), 252. Cf. also his *Theology of the New Testament*, I, 304.

[45] Cf. the essay in reply to Bultmann by Julius Schniewind in *Kerygma and
Myth*, pp. 45 ff.

Some have welcomed Bultmann's program of demythologizing as a great advance over literalism and as a service to the
Christian faith in our time. However, in spite of its merits,
these critics[46] of Bultmann regard demythologizing a for-
feiture. They insist that the mythopoetic language of the New
Testament cannot be translated because myth is the necessary
vehicle for communicating not only about man but about the
universe. Myth conveys a sense of the world, the universal
significance of events. Any translation of mythology into
anthropological categories is therefore regarded as a tragic
reduction.[47] "If the Word of God must necessarily speak
with the mythopoetic words of men, it is all the more inevitable that this should be where the ultimate issues of existence are in question." [48]

While it is generally agreed that the biblical language must
be reckoned with in contemporary theology,[49] the attempt to
save traditional formulations is for many a rather dubious
enterprise.[50] Instead there is—following Bultmann, Tillich,
Bonhoeffer and others—an effort on the part of theology to
relocate transcendence. Pre-existence testifies to transcendence
in temporal and spatial categories that are no longer helpful

---

[46] Lohmeyer, "The Right Interpretation of the Mythological," *Kerygma and
Myth*, pp. 124 ff.; and Wilder, *The Language of the Gospel*, pp. 129 ff.

[47] For a call for a new myth adequate to convey our understanding of reality,
see Leander Keck, *Taking the Bible Seriously* (New York: Association Press,
1962), pp. 114-17.

[48] Wilder, *The Language of the Gospel*, p. 129.

[49] All branches of theology are again struggling with the biblical language
and categories.

[50] John Wren-Lewis, "Does Science Destroy Belief?" p. 39.

and meaningful. The transcendent is now sought in the midst of the world. As Bonhoeffer expressed it, "The transcendent is not infinitely remote, but close at hand." [51] Modern man is secularized, and he has no room for a presentation of the transcendent which appears to him suspiciously like an invitation to otherworldliness, an escape from responsibility in history. "Only the idea of God which can find, which can seek and find, the unconditional in the conditional, the beyond in the here, the transcendent in the present, at hand, as possibility of encounter, is possible for modern man." [52]

But where is this transcendent to be sought and found? It was almost inevitable with the advent of psychology and psychiatry that there would be a tendency to relocate transcendence within this new area of exploration: the human psyche.[53] In fact, a new mythology arose which replaced the cosmic mythology of the New Testament with that of the soul. Id, ego, and superego were the new names for the elemental powers. However, the realm of the subjectivity has proved much too small a canvas for a life-size portrait of the way things really are. The universe of nature, history, and community, not to mention the ambiguous dimension of transcendence, proves to be a world too wide and too real for relocation within the microcosm of the individual.

---

[51] *Prisoner for God*, p. 175.

[52] Bultmann, "The Idea of God and Modern Man," p. 94.

[53] It was inevitable that psychology be viewed by some as the successor of religion, giving rise to countless discussions on the theme. As one article among many see D. A. Pond, "Has Psychiatry Replaced Religion?" *Faith, Fact, Fantasy*, pp. 81 ff.

Following the pioneer work of Martin Buber,[54] some contemporary theologians are relocating transcendence in the depth of interpersonal relationships.[55] The popularity of this direction in theology has been fed by the human community's unhappiness with the increasing depersonalization in an age of technology.

In a much more sophisticated, and therefore less popular, way a number of theologians have attempted to rethink Christology in terms of the process philosophy of Whitehead and Hartshorne. This involves a relocation of transcendence. The mode of thinking expressed in the pre-existence of Christ here requires modification, but transcendence is not eradicated. Neither God nor Christ is to be viewed outside the process of becoming, but the "pre-" and "post-" dimensions of reality are expressed in the primordial and the consummation.[56]

Over against these efforts to reinterpret, relocate, and reformulate transcendence there is a loud protest that such efforts are too conservative of tradition and therefore inadequate for the present time. It is insisted that rather than interpret the *language* of the New Testament so that the

---

[54] *I and Thou*, trans. R. G. Smith (2nd ed.; New York: Scribner, 1958).

[55] Although Buber would not agree with some conclusions drawn by those stimulated by him. John A. T. Robinson has so relocated transcendence (*Honest to God* [Philadelphia: Westminster, 1963], pp. 45-104).

[56] For example, W. Norman Pittenger, *The Word Incarnate* (New York: Harper, 1959), pp. 186-202; J. E. Barnhart, "Incarnation and Process Philosophy," *Religious Studies*, II (1967), 225-32; also T. W. Ogletree, "A Christological Assessment of Dipolar Theism," *Journal of Religion*, XLVII (1967), 87-99.

truth represented by the myth of pre-existence may be understood, there should be raised the clear question of the validity of that truth claim itself. T. J. J. Altizer, a principal spokesman for this new radicality, calls not for a reinterpretation of the pre-existence of Christ but for a rejection of the idea altogether. In fact, no word that appears in nonhistorical form can be accepted as Christian. Therefore, there is absolutely no possibility of mediating to our time the New Testament image of Jesus Christ.[57] Against any claim that this empirical approach reduces Christianity to history, the reply has been that this is no more a reduction of Christianity than astronomy was a reduction of astrology.[58]

Because it raises the question of the truth claims of the Christian faith, this new radical approach[59] calls for a new era in Christian theology. Bultmann and his associates stood within Christian tradition in accepting the Word as *Word of God*; their concern was the communication of that Word to our time. This underlying assumption is now being set aside by a new atheism which rejects all nonhistorical categories. Naturally this includes the rejection of the term and all that is implied by the category of pre-existence.

Of course, there are differences among the radical theologians in the reasons for eliminating transcendence and in the

---

[57] William Hamilton and T. J. J. Altizer, *Radical Theology and the Death of God* (Indianapolis: Bobbs-Merrill, 1966), pp. 122-25.

[58] Paul M. van Buren, *The Secular Meaning of the Gospel* (New York: Macmillan, 1963), p. 198.

[59] I am using "radical" as the term Altizer and Hamilton use to identify their position.

structure of their own formulations.[60] Paul M. van Buren, strongly influenced by linguistic analysis, rejects as meaningless and useless to modern pragmatic man all terminology that refers to transcendent phenomena. The focus of his presentation is Jesus of Nazareth, a man of freedom who lived for his neighbor. Because of his freedom for his neighbor Jesus was killed, but he arose from the dead releasing a power of love and freedom that is universally contagious.[61]

In his formulation van Buren reflects a positive and a negative influence from Karl Barth. Barth framed his own formulation of the Christian faith upon the traditional structures: metaphysical/physical, infinite/finite, eternal/temporal. Influenced by linguistic analysis and its demand for verification, van Buren has "cut off the top half" of Barth's presentation, leaving only the lower half of the dichotomy. He has no room for ideas such as pre-existence because they do not fit into immanence and temporality. Interestingly enough, he has, with the audacity but the opposite perspective of Marcion, extracted from the New Testament the historical Jesus. Then, reminiscent of the "old quest," van Buren portrays this Jesus as one who speaks to modern man because Jesus like modern man affirms freedom and love. Further response to this position will follow shortly.

T. J. J. Altizer's radicality consists, strangely enough, in a

---

[60] For discussions of the differences in the positions of Altizer, Hamilton, and van Buren, cf. T. W. Ogletree, *The Death of God Controversy* (Nashville: Abingdon, 1966), and H. E. Hatt, "A New Trinity: One God in Three Deaths" *Religion in Life*, XXXVI (1967), 53-69.

[61] *The Secular Meaning of the Gospel*, pp. 123-34, 147.

new literalism with reference to New Testament Christology. He accepts a fully kenotic Christology,[62] explaining that the incarnation effects "the absolute negation of the primordial or essential Being of God."[63] Since God is Jesus, transcendence is transformed into immanence.[64] But Altizer's rejection of transcendence is confined to his handling of the divine condescension. The loss of transcendence was a historical phenomenon, but Altizer himself looks for "a contemporary epiphany of Christ."[65] Unlike others who reject all transcendence logically or linguistically, Altizer in a real sense focuses upon it, hoping for a reappearance of Christ. He is not, therefore, a victim of radical historicization, for in his own faith history is relieved by his mysticism.[66] Structurally, his formulation consists of affirming the first two stages of the three-stage motif of Phil. 2:6-11: pre-existence, existence, return (transcendence, immanence, transcendence). Or it might be said that he accepts literally II Cor. 8:9 as the whole story: he who was rich became poor. It is very difficult, therefore, to discover in this death of God the ground for the hope which he seems to manifest. His position is so noticeably autobiographical that readers are unable to probe sufficiently to find answers.[67]

---

[62] *The Gospel of Christian Atheism* (Philadelphia: Westminster, 1966), pp. 44, 68-69, 91.

[63] *Ibid.*, p. 69.

[64] *Ibid.*, p. 113.

[65] *Ibid.*, pp. 9, 132-39.

[66] Hamilton says Altizer "makes empiricists weep" (*The Death of God Controversy*, pp. 30-31).

[67] Avery Dulles, "Some Recent Death-of-God Literature," *Theological Studies,* XXVIII (1967), 111-18.

The literature of this radical theology[68] reflects not only the state of ferment of faith today, but also the reactions against past abuses of religion and abuses by religion. Many of these reactions contain sound indictments against the church, among them the charge that pre-existence has effected docetism and transcendence has produced otherworldliness.

This being admitted, however, the new radicality, like most reactions, contains an error at the other end of the spectrum. It is the error of radical historicization. This probably can best be seen by looking at its opposite, the error of radical dehistoricization expressed in Gnosticism.

Under the pressures from an anxious culture which sought life's meaning in cosmogonic myths and cosmological speculation, Gnostic Christianity turned its back on history. In what was apparently a sincere effort to be meaningful and relevant these Gnostics modified the Christian message without demanding of that culture a modification of its perspective toward historical existence. The one modification without the other created a loss of that tension in the Christian message traditionally expressed in the categories of pre-existence/existence, transcendence/immanence, metahistorical/historical. As a result, Gnosticism's response to culture was a case of the answers sounding exactly like the questions. With the loss of the historical there was the loss of a position from which to evaluate the metahistorical, hence the evaporation of Gnostic Christianity into cosmological mythology.

---

[68] Hamilton's position is not given separately here since a survey of the "God-is-dead" theologians is not my present purpose. For his position and his bibliography see Hatt's article and the book by Ogletree referred to in n. 60.

The current theological position which, by means of extreme historicization, documents the loss or death of the transcendent commits the same error in reverse. In a dialogue with modern Western man, in an effort to be relevant and clear, the new radical theologians turn their backs upon the transcendent. This radical modification without any demand upon culture to modify its perspective results in a loss of tension within theology and hence with culture. Hence, theology does not respond to culture's questions except to join in its anxious laments. By relinquishing the transcendent[69] this perspective becomes captive to unrelieved history because it lacks a stance from which to view and find meaning in history. In what appears to be a very serious view of history there is actually a failure to take history as meaningfully serious as did traditional Christianity with its affirmation of that which transcends history. Apart from a stance outside history there is no way to see meaning within it.[70]

A basic flaw in the approach of this new theology is in its partial attack upon the old dichotomous categories: pre-existence/existence, metahistorical/historical. The attack is not radical enough in that it stands in one half of the dichotomy and denies the other half. Whether one stands in the supranatural and denies history or stands in history and denies the supranatural, the problem is the same. One does not affirm or

---

[69] Langdon Gilkey calls upon the church to testify meaningfully to the transcendent (*How the Church Can Minister to the World Without Losing Itself* [New York: Harper, 1964], esp. ch. 6).

[70] Paul Tillich, *Systematic Theology* (Chicago: University of Chicago Press, 1951), I, 3. Also Gabriel Vahanian, *The Death of God* (New York: George Braziller, 1961), p. 169.

deny half a dichotomy. The problem lies in the inadequacy of the entire motif which understands reality in this way. The radical theologians therefore testify, in the partial nature of their efforts at reorientation, that they are not free of this traditional way of viewing reality.

What is needed is a new mythic structure for understanding reality and for communicating that understanding. The Hellenistic categories, which provided the church with the motif of pre-existence for understanding the ultimate significance of Jesus Christ, have served well but they are no longer adequate. The church is painfully realizing that all ways of structuring her understanding of Christ are provisional. The term "pre-existence" is not sacrosanct and essential to the gospel. Apparently the early church, in the days before doxologies hardened into dogmas and confessions became fixed creeds, understood this. The church adopted this category to convey the meaning of Jesus Christ, and the church can lay it aside for another. This is the meaning this study has sought to convey by reference to "functional" Christology.

To say that the structures upon which Christologies are framed are provisional is not, however, to say that all such structures are adequate. The measure of the proclamation about Jesus Christ is whether or not it is able to communicate the Word which is prior to us and which meets us in our existence. Our history is given meaning by that which surpasses history. An encounter with Jesus Christ is an encounter with God, for his history is revelatory of the Transcendent. Here men stand *coram Deo*. The affirmations of the pre-existence of Christ expressed this central conviction of the faith.

Whether the church will cease to employ temporal and spatial analogies to communicate this dimension of her faith is not yet clear. Perhaps she will. Perhaps new terms—depth, ground, center—will carry this freight of meaning. It is not the purpose of this study either to predict or to suggest. However, it is a clear and firm conclusion of this investigation that to drop the term "pre-existence" without an adequate replacement would be to run the risk of being left with no larger frame of reference for understanding the event of Jesus Christ. This is another way of saying we would be left without a larger frame of reference for understanding human history. The result is almost predictable. Without the overarching (or permeating) presence of the Transcendent, created values cease to be regarded as created; relative values cease to be relative. Just as the lack of a doctrine of creation resulted in ancient man's divinization of the world, the lack of transcendence can result in the absolutizing of history with all its social and political structures. The secularization of the world with all its values begins to be lost as that secularity becomes autonomous. As Bernard Meland has astutely projected:

The common life . . . will suffer a deficiency of spirit that will become delimiting, progressively enclosing its norms and purposes within the demands of the cultural experience. Man's experience then becomes the sole measure of his ways. Men so committed to becoming characteristically human may thus become statically human: that is, a community closed within those established concepts of moral good that the cultural experience can achieve and sustain. What is lost from this social vision is the sense of judgment of challenge that can come from a transcendent measure, or from a sense of limitation in the human structure which will forever keep one open to and inquiring about the validity of human forms and formulations.[71]

In other words, the result would be nihilism.

Because man, not God or Christ, now occupies the center stage of theological discussion, one is not to suppose that there has been a complete change of subject. The starting point in the conversations has shifted, but the Christian faith has always affirmed that there is not a great distance between anthropology and Christology. The incarnation proclaims this. This being the case, there is no more relevant and urgent word to man than Christology. And here in those ancient and strange expressions, "pre-existence" and "postexistence," man finds the raw material for constructing in his own terms the proper perspective for understanding the meaning of his existence. The alternative is to be caught in the inadequacies of degenerate existentialism which holds up a mirror before man. If he likes what he sees, he can indulge in the fleeting joy of narcissism; it not, he may sink into the despair of those preoccupied with the contingency of everything.

---

[71] *The Secularization of Modern Cultures* (New York: Oxford University Press, 1966), p. 126.

Index